BENT
Pages

Anne Hope

ISBN 978-1-63630-206-5 (Paperback)
ISBN 978-1-63630-207-2 (Digital)

Covenant Books, Inc.
11661 Hwy 707
Murrells Inlet, SC 29576
www.covenantbooks.com

Introduction

History is a subject I never relished in school. It seemed boring and inapplicable to my present-day life. How wrong could I have been! History helps determine who we are as an individual, as a family, as a nation, and as a people. So much of who I am, where I am, and what I am is because of what has happened before me…history! It can give us wisdom and identity. It can give us purpose and determination. It can give us hope and faith. We are each part of a larger story. History is not only our individual story, but it is our family's story, our nation's story, our forefather's story. We are all a part of God's big story. He is weaving it to create a masterpiece tapestry. I am but a tiny thread, yet an important thread. Unfortunately, we often lose sight of the larger tapestry and suffer from personal myopia.

History gives us perspective that we can otherwise lose. It gives us a sense of the meaning of life. It gives us a key to who we are, as well as a sense of belonging. Most people, including me, probably haven't thought much about how history affects their lives. Children today rarely remember much history and often think it's boring to learn. Yet if they don't know the history of the Beatles, how could they possibly understand the baby boomer generation? If they don't understand the history of the Vietnam War, how could they understand the reluctance of Americans to get involved in foreign wars? If they don't understand the Holocaust and Jewish history, how can they understand what is happening in the Middle East today? When visiting Israel, I was envious of how even young children could recite facts of Jewish history. I'm not sure my own daughter could remember many major facts within the last few hundreds of years that have made our nation what it is today. I'm not even sure I could! There are probably many Americans who are not even aware our nation was founded primarily due to individuals seeking religious freedom. Much of our constitution and founding principles were based on the hunger for this freedom.

I am who I am partly because I was born in America, into a southern culture, into a low-income household to parents who divorced during a time period when divorce was frowned upon. I am who I am partly because I grew up without a father and with a mother who had many problems, health and otherwise. I am who I am partly because I had grandparents and aunts and uncles who cared. I am who I am because I had a pastor, teachers, and coaches who took an interest in me and mentored me. My personality was influenced by the many colloquialisms with which I grew up. "Whistling girls and cackling hens always come to some bad end." "Good girls don't drink, smoke, or dance, and don't date boys who do." "Dirty laundry stays in the family…we don't discuss those things." "God helps those who help themselves, and God honors modesty." "Early to bed, early to rise, makes a person healthy, wealthy, and wise." "Cracking your knuckles, burping, and passing gas is unladylike." "You don't talk back to adults, and you don't curse." "Don't let others see you cry." "Don't hang around with people from divorced homes. They are a bad influence." "Pretty is as pretty does."

So I didn't whistle, drink, smoke, burp, pass gas, crack my knuckles (except when my brother tortured me with it), talk back to adults, curse, discuss family laundry, or cry in public. I didn't have to worry about dating guys who did since I rarely dated until I left home for college. I didn't have to worry about who I hung around with since most people avoided me because I was from a divorced family. I did dance, however, and rarely went to bed early. I'm sure that is much of the reason why I am not particularly healthy, wealthy, or wise. I grew up in the baby boomer age, Beatles, rock and roll, and drugs. I grew up during the time when sirens went off at various times during the week, and all the children at school were required to get under their desks to practice for a nuclear attack. (As if that would help!) My mother worked for the government in the area of special

4

warfare and was very secretive. She knew about the Bay of Pigs plan and couldn't tell us. She sent us off to school that morning with tears in her eyes, telling us, "If the warning siren goes off today, do *every-thing* the teacher says to do." Somehow, I associated her secretiveness with a deep distrust for government. It probably didn't help that my grandmother swore we never really sent a man to space. She was certain it was all just a publicity stunt with special effects.

Growing up, we ate mostly what we grew. Thus, I had never set eyes on broccoli, asparagus, cauliflower, Brussels sprouts, spinach, papaya, mango, and other exotic foods until I went to college. I had never tasted alcohol, never even seen or smelled illegal drugs, and had never even seen a picture of a naked man or woman. How often does a girl go to college these days and not realize that men have pubic hair? How different I might have turned out if I had been French, drank wine with my meals, and went to nude beaches in the summer on the Riviera! Or what if I had grown up in South Africa and experienced apartheid? What if I had been born on a remote island and never knew the joy of rock and roll?

Indeed, our history helps determine much of who we are and what we become. It helps us explain and comprehend our biases, our fears, and our insecurities. The one thing I knew beyond a shadow of a doubt was that I wanted my daughter's history to be different than mine. I did not want history to repeat itself as it often tends to do! I wanted her to know unconditional love. I wanted her to have me there when she needed me. I wanted her to grow up knowing and loving God, feeling secure in who and what she was in her environment. Little did I know that in seeking to provide those things for her, I would change and grow so very much myself. Just as 911 used to mean nine hundred and eleven when I was a child, due to circumstances and history, it changed to mean nine-one-one when I was a young adult...a number you call when there is an emergency. And then the meaning changed once again when I was middle-aged to mean nine eleven, an act of terror. So it was that I evolved, and the meaning of so many things changed when viewed through the eyes of parenthood. Little did I know that providing unconditional love to my child would, in return, bless me with an incredible healing of reciprocal unconditional love. How could I have known that sacrificing for my child would bring a peace and pleasure and fulfillment of so many dreams? How could I have known that a tiny hand placed in mine could make me feel more secure than ever in my life? Parenthood was a burst of unexpected grace!

The experiences of parenthood helped me understand all the seemingly unreasonable biblical paradoxes. Paradoxes challenge us; they create tension in us. They seem to be wrong when we first hear them, leaving us striving to wrap our minds around their truth. Yet as we grow in faith and test them, their veracity can be clearly seen. Rather than confuse us, they give us wisdom.

- It is in giving that we receive.
- The weak shall be strong.
- The humble shall be exalted.
- There is freedom through servitude.
- We can gain the whole world yet lose our souls.
- We must come to the end of ourselves to find ourselves.
- The more we die to self, the more we can actually live abundantly in Christ.
- Even if I lose every material possession, I am rich in Christ.
- Give and it will be given to you.
- The last will be made first.
- We are in the world, but not of it.
- To live, you must die.
- Surrender your life to save it.
- Difficulties are a reason for joy.
- True leadership is found in serving.

This journey of life with all its hills, valleys, cliffs, and snares actually helped me discover that the biblical guide to joy is real and true. The trek of parenthood kept me dependent of God more than I ever could have imagined. The beatitudes came alive! The poor in spirit *will* experience the kingdom of heaven. Those who mourn *will* be comforted. The meek *will* inherit the earth. Those who hunger and thirst for righteousness *will* be filled. The merciful *will* be shown mercy. The pure in heart *will* see God. The peacemakers *will* be called the children of God. And those who are persecuted for righteousness' sake, theirs *will* be the kingdom of heaven.

As I look back on my life, I see the fulfillment of each of these. I see the true joy and blessings that I've experienced. And I am so very grateful! I see that I am playing a role in history. I have a purpose. I can make an impact. God has wired me specifically with certain talents, abilities, and personality traits when he knit me together in my mother's womb. I long to fulfill my role in his plan for history. I have discovered that I can make a difference, one person at a time, beginning with me. I have learned that God is indeed in control. Although there are still many times I want to be in control, I have learned that when I give in to that desire, I forfeit faith. I have found the two cannot coexist. When I want to control things, I relinquish faith. And there is great danger and risk in relinquishing faith. When I think long and hard about it, I trust God a lot more than I trust myself! Through events in my life, I have learned that to give up that control is the ultimate joy, the ultimate peace.

But giving up that control is a daily battle. It is a war within myself. During the battles, it helps me to remember the past. Just as God's Word continually admonished the Israelites to remember their past and recall all he had done for them, I can look back and see all the ways God has protected me, led me, loved me, and provided for me. As time passes, I often see past experiences take on a new meaning. What was once devastating and difficult to understand is now a blessing. What was once shameful is now a strength and a tool. What was once a devastating disappointment is now clearly viewed as a protection. To be able to let go and trust that God has a future and a hope for my good and for the benefit of his plan is freeing. It's a historical lesson I hope to impart to my child and to those who come to know me as I remember all the ways God has protected me, guided me, provided for me, and loved me as his child.

From the time I was a child, one of my habits that drove others in my family crazy was to bend the corner of a page down on a book I was reading if it contained information I wanted to remember and look back on. It was easy to tell which books I had read and had been inspired by…there would be many bent corners. This book is a snapshot of bent corners of pages in my life that have inspired and taught me. They are moments I never want to forget, even if it's painful. They have made me who I am. They are my history. And I wouldn't change that for the world!

Perhaps it is just as important that I have learned I get to choose how I want to view history. I can choose to be a victim. I can choose to be angry. Or I can choose to be a victor…a person who chooses joy in seeing the gracious hand of God creating a beautiful symphony to share with others as part of his great plan. I want to sing him a love song…my life, the melody. Welcome to the adventure!

Chapter 1

It was Saint Patrick's Day, and there was a good reason to celebrate. I was having a baby. It was twelve fifteen in the afternoon, and I was in the delivery room with my husband, surrounded by the doctors and nurses. It was to be a C-section. The baby was large, and I had a lung infection. They were taking the baby two weeks early. I had had no labor and not much discomfort other than feeling like a whale.

My husband and I had chosen not to find out the sex of the baby. We wanted to be surprised. Actually, I didn't care so much about being surprised; I just didn't want to deal with everyone on the paternal side of the family who desperately wanted a boy. Somehow, I just had an intuition that it was probably going to be a girl. I didn't particularly want to deal with any disappointment from them if we found out early it was a girl. I decided I would just deal with it when the time came. There was certainly enough to deal with already without heaping on any more stress.

We had planned a wedding for the summer, but at the last minute decided to simplify and have a very small wedding on the beach. The stress of family disagreements concerning wedding plans got to both of us, and we caved. A fast, simple wedding with just a few family and friends was easier. Of course, when wedding plans are dumped, there can always be the assumption that there *must* be a reason why the couple decided to speed up the wedding and throw away the lavish plans. So as time passed, I could *feel* the stinging suspicion. It certainly didn't help that I got pregnant on the honeymoon. I could almost hear people counting the days until the baby was born.

When we married, the decision had been made that I was not going to use birth control pills. We weren't all that young, and we were both fine with the idea that it would happen when it happens, but I *had* planned to be careful. And I thought I was. What happened on the honeymoon cruise did not stay on the cruise; it stayed in my belly. And it seemed from the beginning, we were on a disaster course. It's good we don't know what is in store for us down the road. To believe we could endure it would stretch the imagination beyond comprehension at the time.

The Caribbean honeymoon cruise turned sour when I got a parasite from something I ate. By the time we returned to the states, I was severely dehydrated and could barely keep my head up. I had thrown up for two days straight. I'm not sure I had ever felt worse. They had to force me off the boat as I didn't think I could walk. I laid prostrate on the floor of the airport, unsure if I could even stand to board the plane. The trip home was a nightmare. The next day, I went to the doctor, and it's like I had every test imaginable run.

It took a couple of days for all the test results to come back. When the doctor called me to come back in, he informed me it was state law to administer a pregnancy test prior to prescribing the antidote for the parasite. Permission was granted as I was sure I could not be pregnant. You can imagine my surprise when the nurse called the next day and said, "Congratulations, you're pregnant!" I burst out crying. I wasn't sure I was ready to be a parent, regardless of what I had previously thought. Is anyone really ready to be a parent? I had not even learned to be a wife! On top of that, the doctor could not give me the heavy-duty medication to rid me of the parasite. He put me on a regimen of a lower dose, but he was afraid even that small dose could be harmful to the fetus. Yet there seemed to be little choice.

Two weeks after finding out I was pregnant, I returned from a work trip on a Sunday night. My husband picked me up from the airport and took me to dinner. I was still feeling very nauseous and had very little desire to be in front of food. But going out was better than cooking! After the meal, he turned his collar down and asked,

"Honey, what do you think this is?" On his lower neck was a large bulbous tumor.

Fear gripped me, and I immediately responded, "I don't know what it is, but it is *not* good…and we are going to the doctor tomorrow morning."

We got in to see the doctor the next morning. His reaction to seeing the bulging tumor was exactly like mine…it was not good. The doctor arranged for a biopsy that afternoon, and we had the long two-day wait for the pathology report to come back. My guess was Hodgkin's. But to the surprise of everyone, it came back as testicular cancer that had already advanced, with secondary tumors in the abdomen and lungs. The visible tumor in the neck was the tip of a large tumor protruding from the chest cavity. We were stunned by the news.

The doctor, however, was hopeful and gave us a prognosis of a 70 percent survival rate. Although the cancer was quite advanced, the doctor explained there had been great strides in treating testicular cancer in recent years. He laid out the chemotherapy treatments that would be required, as well as the surgeries and tests that were projected for the future. It was to be a long road to recovery. My husband, the father of my child, was only twenty-six years old. The doctor recommended that we visit a sperm bank if we intended to try to have additional children since after the chemotherapy, my husband would be sterile.

*****

The first surgery was scheduled for the following day to remove the testicle in which the cancer had originated. The surgery went well, and the next day, the doctor talked with us about the sperm bank results. To our dismay, he stated the sperm was already mutated, and the health of the baby I was now carrying may not be good. The medical team suspected malformations in the fetus. He recommended aborting and informed us that the lab had found no viable sperm in the sample. We discussed testing, abortion (not an option for me), and how to proceed. The doctor seemed to be very disappointed and worried that we chose not to abort. I felt like the gift of life that had been given to us was precious. It was a gift from God. There was no way I was destroying that…for better or for worse. We chose not to do testing. If there were defects, I did not want to know about them just then. Maybe I was in a state of denial. I chose to believe it was faith…that prayers would be answered. Now it was a waiting game…on all sides.

The chemotherapy regimen was aggressive. He spent five days in the hospital on intravenous chemotherapy, then five to seven days of throwing up, and finally three to five days of feeling somewhat human. This pattern went on for the next eleven months. It was a brutal year! The plan was to get the cancer count in the blood down to zero and operate on the remaining tumors. The sickness, depression, weight loss, hair loss, and feeling like your masculinity had been ripped from you turned my husband into a man I didn't know. These were long, long months of sadness, insecurity, loneliness, and fear for both of us. The most alone I have ever felt was in my marriage at this time.

My husband was quickly unable to work, and I became the main breadwinner. I'm not sure who threw up more…me or my husband. I had morning sickness throughout the pregnancy, but especially so during the first two months when I was still trying to rid my body of the parasite. When I wasn't cleaning up vomit, I was working and trying to adjust to all the changes that happen to your body during pregnancy. My husband was feeling ugly from the effects of chemotherapy; I was feeling uglier. I was feeling sick; he was feeling sicker. We were both feeling more alone and desperate than we'd ever felt in our lives…like children that had somehow been abandoned.

We each dealt with the situation in our own way, often in unhealthy ways. Rather than draw closer, we drew further apart. Angry words were said. Hurtful actions occurred. One day, I came home from work to find an empty house that was just a mess. I was so tired of working each day, coming home to a house I had to clean, and feeling nauseous from the pregnancy. My patience and temper were wearing thin. For each of us, it was "all about me." Neither of us was mature enough or selfless enough to bear the strain gracefully.

Chapter 2

Had my history been different, perhaps I would have been able to handle the situation a bit better. Who knows how one will react under extreme duress until the situation presents itself? I'm certain I had not developed all the tools needed at that time to undergo such trauma gracefully. Unconditional and selfless love was still a foreign concept to me.

A friend of mine, a psychiatrist, once told me that if he could get a person to write down their ten earliest memories, he could gain a pretty good understanding of how that person had become the man or woman he or she was. And if he could get that person to then write down what they felt their top ten most important decisions had been in their life, he felt he could gain an insight into what decisions that person might need to make in the future to change the course of their life for the better. I set out to examine those memories and decisions for myself.

Looking back is a risk. It can be painful. It can dredge up things that you never wanted to think about again. But I felt deep in my heart that if I was to change the course of history for my daughter, it was something that needed to be done. Change is a decision, and I wanted to make decisions wisely, even if it meant examining parts of my history that were painful or blurry. To my delight, many memories also brought laughter and a new sense of appreciation for the difficulties we all face in growing up in our microcosmic worlds. We all start out as children with it being "all about me," and we view our microcosms only through those eyes that are focused on ourselves at the time. Events can take on a meaning that we, as children, glean to mean one thing. Yet as we grow and mature, we are often able to view those experiences and the people involved in a whole new light... sometimes even as unexpected blessings.

I had grown up in a small town in the south. Divorce in this Southern Baptist community was extremely uncommon. Coming from a broken home seemed to indicate strongly to many others at the time that those children coming from a divorced family were broken as well. I resented that! Little did I know when I was growing up that everyone is broken in some way. At the time, I seemed to be surrounded by perfect families with no shattered glass littering their lives.

My father left when I was eighteen months old, never to return. My mother suffered with severe depression and prescription drug addiction for most of her adult life, surviving multiple suicide attempts. It seemed the old adage was true for my brother and I... the "village" did raise us in many ways. My mother was barely able to look after herself at times. Grandparents, aunts and uncles, cousins, and caring neighbors were a major part of my childhood.

Momma worked long hours for the federal government and drove about an hour to work each day. She was brilliant. In fact, I'm pretty sure I am the least intelligent in our small nucleus family. She had an extremely high IQ but seemed to be lacking in common sense at times. There was the time when she placed the boiling pot of potatoes from the burner onto the Formica counter and set the kitchen on fire. She wasn't much of a cook and tended to burn things. Most of the time, our pancakes were runny because she didn't want to burn them. I became rather fond of runny pancakes and, to my friends' disgust, still prefer them that way when I cook. She did have her specialties—hamburger gravy and chocolate cake with pecans. Other than that, it was hit or miss.

One Thanksgiving, several of the extended family were invited to Thanksgiving dinner. Momma spent the whole day cooking. I spent the whole day worrying if anything would be edible. Thankfully, it was a bit of a potluck with some side dishes being provided by others. The table was lovely. The very large turkey looked delicious. We stood around the table, held hands, and gave thanks for the meal and for family. Then it was time to carve the turkey. With the knife and fork poised above the turkey, much to do was made on carving the pretty bird. We all watched as the knife moved back and forth with little progress. More pressure was added. Was it a dull knife? My cousin, Sara, knew the cooking intelligence of my mother and asked, "Aunt Doris, did you cook it long enough?"

Momma replied, "Yes, I cooked it seven hours, just like it said to."

With a brief pause, Sara then posed the question, "Did you thaw it first?"

The turkey was still frozen solid for the most part. It's hard to tell how Momma felt about that fiasco. She never revealed much. To others, she was always the life of the party. Not many knew the demons that haunted her. She saved that for my brother and me.

*****

I don't remember an awful lot about my childhood, but certain moments stand out. Perhaps selective memory kicks in for those times that seemingly form us. We grew up rather poor but always had enough on the table. I had coffee and bacon for breakfast for as long as I can remember...and I'm still alive! Go figure. I probably would have been six feet tall had I not had coffee every day. After all, we *all* know coffee stunts the growth of children! In the summer, I had fatback (100 percent fried pork fat on the rind) almost every day at lunch with fried corn bread. It's a wonder my arteries are not completely blocked! I still love the smell of pork fat!

My first memory was when I was eighteen months old. I had no idea I was that young, but when I relayed the memory to Momma as an adult, she was floored. It was hard for her to believe all the details I could recall of the memory from that young an age. It's the one and only memory I have of my father. He was taking us to visit his mother in Chattanooga, Tennessee, where he was then working. My parents were already separated at that time. It may have been the last time I saw him. We drove from North Carolina over the Appalachian Mountains. As we crossed the mountains that night in my dad's large red convertible, a snowstorm hit. I can remember the wipers freezing.

We had to stop on the side of the road because the windshield would not clear any longer with the wipers. Dad decided we would sleep in the car until the snowstorm passed. My brother slept in the back seat with my dad's coat over him, and I slept cuddled with my dad in the front…the heat from his body kept me warm. The next morning, the snow had stopped falling. Dad cleaned the car off, and we continued on our way.

Dad was living with his mother, my grans, at the time. The house in Chattanooga had a brick wall around it and a wide front porch. I can remember running out on the front porch and seeing lizards run up and down the wall. I'd scream and run back in the house. It was a game the lizards and I would play. They terrified me, so I wanted to terrify them back by screaming. My dad would go to work later in the day. He was a radio disc jockey. Elvis was a big deal at the time. My grandmother would gather my brother and I around the radio each night to listen to my dad on the station. Then at a certain time each night, he would take the time to say, "And now, it's time for Anne and Gary to go to sleep." We'd wait for those words, and my grandmother would put us down for the night.

I don't remember much else until I was three or four years old. My mom had moved to Virginia for a job. She couldn't afford to take care of both children, so my brother stayed with my aunt, and I moved with my mother. My aunt used to put my brother on a train at times, and he would travel alone as a six-year-old up to Virginia to visit. There are fleeting memories during some of those visits. We lived near a pastor who had an older son; he must have been about twelve years old. He was a *lot* bigger. His mom would babysit me, and we played at their house. There was a pony once. I don't know if they owned the pony or rented it for the day, but we got to ride it. My brother was there for one Halloween, and my mother forced my brother and the pastor's son to take me trick-or-treating. We would run from house to house. It was dark, and I always felt they were trying to run away from me. I struggled to keep up. They got so far ahead of me at one point that I cut across a yard, running full speed to catch up to them on the sidewalk. I didn't see the very thin wire that had been placed around the property to prevent kids on the grass. I ran full speed into the wire, slicing my throat. My screaming brought my brother to the rescue. Needless to say, the fun was over for the night as I was delivered back home with blood running down the front of me, staining my shirt, looking as though someone had slit my throat.

One time, after my brother returned to North Carolina, I was at the pastor's house for the day during a babysitting stint. I rarely ever ate candy; we just couldn't afford it. I had never had chocolate M&M's in my life. I loved chocolate. I couldn't read yet, but I *knew* when I saw that unopened bag on the kitchen counter what was in that bag. I couldn't take my eyes off it. The pastor's son watched me as I stared at the bag. I was so hoping that he would offer some to me. After what seemed like the longest time, he asked, "Do you want some M&M's?"

I was so excited I couldn't speak. I just nodded my head vigorously. Very quietly, he approached me and whispered in my ear, "If you take off your clothes in the shed out back and run around the shed twice, I'll give you the whole bag." I took the candy and ran. And the shame of it haunted me well into adulthood.

The next time my brother came to visit, we were scheduled to stay with the pastor's family again for a babysitting stint. I never wanted to go to that house again. I packed my one purple suitcase and put my toy phonograph in it. That was all that would fit. I wanted my family to know I was serious about this running away stuff. I made it as far as three blocks and got tired of carrying the small suitcase. I hid in the bushes for what seemed like hours. Momma sent my brother to look for me. I'm not sure anyone was that worried. A four-year-old wasn't going to get far, and that was probably before child abduction was so prevalent. My brother eventually found me in the bushes. He laughed very hard and long and ushered me home. It was humiliating! Thank goodness we relocated back to North Carolina soon after that.

We moved in with my maternal grandparents, and I entered school. I was excited to begin school and meet friends, but it didn't turn out quite the way I had hoped. I can remember running out of class with a new schoolmate one day. Her mother was picking her up from school, and she asked her mom if I could come home with her and play. Right in front of me, the mother responded, "I don't think so, honey…she comes from a divorced home." I felt so dejected and branded.

I never did have many friends in school. I never had a birthday party with friends at it. After begging her, Momma did throw me a birthday party when I turned eight. No one came. There were no other birthday parties, except for family. Each birthday, my aunt would give me two new dresses to last me for the year. They were always big at first, but by the end of the year, I grew into and out of them.

The feeling of inadequacy spurred me to become a perfectionist and overachiever. I thought if I could only be good enough and achieve great things, people would then like and respect me. I was nice to people. I was a very good athlete. I excelled in the classroom, yet I never felt accepted. Nor did I ever feel I had true friends.

I didn't even think my teachers really liked me. In the third grade, I was so sick I could barely lift my head off my desk. My stomach was killing me. The teacher kept yelling at me to lift my head and "stop faking it." I kept telling her I was sick. She kept telling me to pay attention.

At the end of the day, the classroom emptied…all except me. The teacher told me to get up and go home, to which I replied, "I can't."

By that time, I couldn't even walk. She was so angry. She called my aunt to come get me since my mother was working. I was rescued by my aunt, who called the doctor when I got home. That was back when doctors actually did house calls in a small town. Unfortunately for me, small town doctors are not always the best. He merely gave me an enema and said, "She should be fine…that will teach her to fake a stomachache."

By the time Momma got home, I had a raging fever and was throwing up. She drove me thirty miles to the closest city with a hospital. My appendix had burst, and the doctors had to do emergency surgery. I was in the hospital four days. I now only remember that hospital experience as being good. My mom was there, my teacher came and apologized, and I got ice cream every day.

*****

My world seemed to fall apart in the next few years. The Cold War was at its height. Nuclear threat was real. The warning sirens would go off regularly. We would crawl under our desks at school and wait on shaking hands and knees. No one was sure if the warning was real or not until several minutes later when the clear siren would sound. We all lived in terror that our world was about to end. I'm not sure what use the siren was, except to terrorize everyone. There was no nuclear shelter in our town, and I'm quite certain those desks were not going to save our lives.

In 1963, President Kennedy was assassinated, and Momma struggled through her first of several suicide attempts. The failed attempt brought on a lengthy stay at a mental hospital for her. I didn't see her for months while they did electroshock treatments on her and tried to make her better. There weren't many good treatments for depression at that time. My brother and I were separated again during this time, each going to separate homes. Momma never seemed to be the same after that. Even after her return home, she struggled with depression. At times, I would go days without seeing her. She would come home so late at night and get up before I was awake in the morning. As we grew older, there were times she didn't come home at all.

Momma was beautiful and vivacious on the outside. She did modeling on the side. Her platinum blonde hair, perfect skin, patrician features, long legs, and shapely figure made her stand out in any crowd. She wore high heels like a badge of honor. Very few would know she was struggling with depression. She was very good at hiding things…especially her thoughts and emotions. Most of my brother's friends had a crush on her. My brother looked a lot like her, and I just couldn't figure out how she could have a child like me…freckled, redheaded, with a head full of cowlicks. I thought I must have been adopted as I was seemingly the ugly duckling of the family. To me, that just meant I had to be better at everything to compensate!

I had no concept of selfless love as a child. I didn't see it modeled. I only knew self-preservation. Childhood was an exercise in survival to me. There seemed to be no chance to enjoy those years growing up. I was alone much of the time, living in my own dreamworld, trying to figure a way out of the chaos of my life. And I was angry, so very angry most of the time. I just wanted to escape. I felt if I could just be good enough and excel in school, it would open the door to the world where no one would know my past. No one would judge me based on my family situation, and the shame would disappear. Everything I did, for the most part, was geared toward escape.

I walked home from school each day by myself in those early years. On the way home, I passed a Baptist church that seemed to always be open. I started going in there to escape the heat and humidity or the wind and cold. Each day, I peeped in through the door to see if anyone was in the sanctuary. Rarely was there anyone there. If not, I slipped quietly in and laid down on the floor underneath a pew. As I laid there, I would whisper to God. He was always very real to me. He was my one true friend that never let me down. I don't know why I felt that way. At the time, our family did not really attend church. But somehow, I knew God was always there, and somehow, I felt closer to him lying there on the floor underneath that pew. Each time I visited, God and I would have these conversations. They weren't holy conversations. I would just tell him about my day, my worries, my fears, my home run in kickball…it all seemed very normal to me. I felt his presence. I knew beyond a shadow of a doubt that he was listening. And then, I would lie there to see if he'd tell me anything. I would hear his laughter, his joy, and feel his love for me. It was so very real.

I think Momma took us to church on holidays, but I really can't remember. I had seen pictures of Momma and me dressed in our Easter bonnets and assumed we had to have worn them somewhere…most likely to church. I remember asking my grandfather to take me to that Baptist church when I was seven. My grandparents were invalids and really didn't get out of the house much. But the

Baptist church was near their house, and Granddaddy could walk around town with the best of them! Although he had suffered a stroke that left him paralyzed on his right side, each day, he would try to walk all around town. I learned from him there were treasures to be found if you walked around looking at the ground. He would always return with nickels, dimes, quarters, and pennies that he had found. He kept a coin collection, which was divided up when he died. I still have my portion and treasure it! It's probably not worth anything, but it was a part of Granddaddy.

One Sunday morning, Granddaddy took me to the big service at the Baptist church. It was rather scary with all the people in it and took a while to get used to, but we continued to go, and eventually my mom and brother started going as well. Sunday school was a haven. I felt accepted for the first time. The teachers were so kind. The pastor even visited my grandparents' house each week! So it was that I learned all about Jesus and God and the selfless love God has for the world, but it was head knowledge. I knew in my head that Jesus loved me enough to die for me. But until I had my own child, I'm not sure if I would have ever understood exactly what that meant. I didn't feel that any human I knew loved me enough to die for me. In fact, my family wasn't demonstrative or vocal with love at all. I don't even remember my mother telling me she loved me until I was twenty-four years old.

Some of that may have been because I was so angry most of the time. I was angry because I was poor and from a divorced home. I was angry because I had to wear the same clothes several times a week. I was angry because I had no friends. I was very angry that others saw me as someone to be pitied or avoided. I was angry that I had red hair and freckles. I was angry that my mother had a stigma for having been in a mental institution. I was angry that I had to sleep in the same bed with my mother, and I would wake up with banana slices in the bed and peanut butter smeared on the sheet when she had fallen asleep eating in bed. I was angry because she didn't come home and spend time with me. I was angry that she didn't even bother to come home some days. I was angry when she got addicted to pain medication. I was angry when she would beat me with a belt or a switch from the bush outside the house when I made her angry, but that was a time when most parents spanked their children to discipline them. That finally stopped when I was fourteen. I don't even remember what I did to warrant the punishment. Perhaps I had flushed her pills down the toilet. Whatever the reason, she made me pull down my pants and bend over the bed. I was resigned that day not to cry at all costs. I was too angry to cry. She proceeded to beat me with the belt buckle until I was bleeding, and she was crying. Collapsing on the floor in tears, she looked up at me tearfully. I pulled my pants back up, turned around, and with as much rage and hurt as I could muster, I informed her in no uncertain terms, "If you ever hit me again, I'll kill you." At the time, I think I meant it. And she never hit me again. But she didn't have much else to do with me either.

Chapter 3

The nine months of pregnancy went by slowly. Nausea and heartburn plagued me throughout. I had so much trouble eating protein. My doctor kept telling me I had to force myself because protein was important to the brain development of the baby. So if the baby turned out to be stupid, it was certainly going to be my fault!

When I didn't self-abort during the first three months, I felt a certainty that God had answered my prayer for a healthy child. I didn't want to have an amniocentesis, and I still didn't want to know the sex of the child. I didn't want to decorate a room, and I didn't want to buy presents. I had enough trouble just functioning each day.

We had decided on a name if it was to be a boy, but had no ideas for a girl. The boy was to be Michael David—not very original. I'm sure if it had been a boy, I would have wished in the long run that I had named him something much cooler, like Jonah or Caleb or Bryce. Bryce would not have gone over well with my brother since all names should be at least two syllables according to him to be cool. It seemed I was the only one who contemplated a possible girl's name since everyone else seemed convinced it was to be a boy. My six-year-old niece asked one day what the baby would be named if it was a girl. I said, "I really don't know. Do you have a suggestion?"

She replied, "How's about my baby doll's name, Jessica?"

She carried that baby everywhere with her; it was so beat-up. I didn't have the heart to tell her I didn't really like that name, but I think she picked up on it just the same. Kids are like that. When I didn't give her an immediate response, she added, "But I think I might name my next baby doll, Casey!" Now *that* one struck a chord.

Casey it was! I rather liked unisex names for girls. It had an Irish ring to it, and being a tomboy myself, I could just picture her…Casey at bat!

Pregnancy seemed to drag on with more and more stress. Although I treasured my pregnancy and talked regularly to the baby, the sadness and stress were overwhelming. The baby seemed to be the only thing keeping me going. The chemotherapy treatments continued throughout for my husband, with both of us becoming increasingly depressed. One evening, I came home from work to find my husband huddled over the heat vent in the living room using a blanket as a tent to capture the heat. He was always cold. The lights were off, and it was dark. He was sitting there, crying. I waddled over and eased myself down on the floor next to him, putting my arms around him. I wanted so badly to comfort him. We sat there for several minutes until he looked up at me with tears streaking down his face and said, "I'm so miserable…I don't love you…I don't want to be here…and I don't have anywhere else to go." I felt like a boulder had fallen on me.

The logical part of my brain wanted to believe it was the chemotherapy and depression talking. But I was a hormonal mess…a large pregnant woman who was feeling ugly enough with a gigantic stomach and puffy face. A part of me wanted to hit him. A part of me wanted to throw him out. In the long run, I just hugged him harder and said, "It's okay…you're my husband and the father of our baby. You can stay here as long as you like, and you can move into the other bedroom if it makes you feel better. I'll look after you." He stood up and began to move his things into the spare bedroom.

Several weeks later, I was cleaning the house and found a letter on top of the refrigerator (of all places). The letter was open, and it was addressed to my husband from a woman. Perhaps I shouldn't have read it. After all, it wasn't addressed to me. Perhaps he left it there for me to find because he didn't know how to tell me. My husband was seeing another woman.

He was in the hospital, getting chemotherapy treatments at the time. When I went to the hospital the next day, I confronted him with the letter. His sobs made me feel no better. He tried to explain that he didn't feel like a man any longer and wanted to see if he could still function. All I could do was feel sorry for myself. I don't even know if I felt anger any longer…just sadness and depression. Even my husband could not love me. Could anyone?

It brought back so many memories…memories of feeling unloved by those who should be teaching you love and acceptance. Where was that someone to tell you that you are brave, you are loved, you are worthy, and you are respected? All I could remember was rejection…rejection from the community, rejection from classmates, rejection from family. I felt damaged. I was desperate not to hate my background while all the time craving love from those very people who helped create that background.

So many memories…I can clearly remember those times when my mother would come home late and just wanted to sit on the couch and read. I merely wanted to be close to her. As she sat on the couch, reading, I would put my head in her lap. She would push me away and ask me to leave her alone. Or there was the time I had asked her to come to my award's ceremony when I won the president's speech award. She never showed, although she promised. She didn't even come home that night. To be fair, I'm sure I caused her a great deal of frustration. To me, as a child, love was spelled T-I-M-E. I would pitch a fit when she didn't come home at night. All I wanted was to spend time with her. I was so very lonely. I just wanted to feel love. Yet it seemed to push her further away. She was dealing with her own demons. There are demons in all of us. It would take me a long time to learn that the first step to loving someone is to recognize and deal with my own demons so that I can understand and forgive others.

Those demons dragged her further and further into herself. She just didn't seem to have much to give when she got home. When I was a teenager, Momma was diagnosed with lymphatic leukemia. Once again, she had to go away for a while. She was hospitalized and getting treatments at a specialized hospital three hours away. It didn't take long for her to become addicted to pain medication. It wasn't unusual for me to find prescriptions for the same medication issued by different doctors at the same time. There were many times when she would pass out, often at inconvenient times—the middle of din-ner at a restaurant, a sporting event, a party. It was embarrassing to me and made me even more angry. I just couldn't understand addic-tion at the time. And she couldn't understand why I seemingly tor-tured her with surliness, complaints, and senseless anger. There were times when I would flush the pills down the toilet or throw them out the car window on a long drive. That only created a vicious cycle of my anger with Momma and her anger with me. The relationship did not seem to improve for many years.

Chapter 4

Finally, the day arrived. The doctor decided to take the baby early since I had a lung infection that was getting progressively worse. The birth date was to be Saint Patrick's Day! What better day to have an Irish baby, and it was scheduled for a day when my husband was off chemo for a while. At noon that day, I was ushered into the delivery room and administered a spinal block. My husband, who fainted at the mere smell of a hospital, was at the head of the bed. I wasn't sure he would make it through the birth in a conscious state. Within minutes, chaos erupted. The incision was made; the baby's head popped out of my abdominal wall and started screaming. It was like an alien hanging out of my stomach, making my husband immediately faint. The nurses raced to catch him. The doctor was holding the baby's head, waiting to pull the rest of the body out. I sat up on my elbows and watched the whole thing unfold like a comedy. "Congratulations...you have a girl!" But I was the only one who heard it as my husband lay unconscious on the floor.

She was adored from the moment any family member laid eyes on her. She was a large baby, ten pounds when she was born. Her onion head with the tuft of orange-red hair on top, her perfect peachy skin, and the dimples in her chin and cheeks made her irresistible. Her father swaddled her, talked to her, dozed with her, and bragged about her from the moment he saw her. My main question was, "Is she healthy?"

Much to my relief, she checked out perfectly! When the doctor was cleaning up the wound, he relayed to me how fearful he had been about her health. He told me he had been dreading the birth. He was exuberant and insisted she was a miracle baby. I was happy to accept that explanation. I felt God had been looking out for us all along! This was meant to be.

We were in the hospital for several days…me for three, Casey for four. On the first day, the nurse tried to get me up out of bed. I tried to resist, telling the nurse how nauseous I was. She wrapped her arms around me and pulled me up out of bed. I promptly threw up all over her. I won! She laid me back down until the next day.

Casey developed jaundice on the second day and had to be placed under sunlamps several times a day. Her skin was a golden brown. Her huge blue eyes popped out at you. I held her for long periods each day, sitting in a rocker. I can vividly remember the awe, and for the first time in my life, I understood. I now knew what it was like to love someone enough to die for her. What I had known in my head, that crazy love God has for man, I could now understand in my heart. It was now so very personal and so very overwhelming.

Going home without my baby was tough. I didn't want to leave her. She was now my lifeline to get through this storm of life, but she needed to stay an extra day for jaundice treatment. Leaving the hospital, I cried. Walking into the house, my husband immediately went to the bathroom, didn't make it in time and threw up all over the floor and bathtub. Without even making it to the bedroom, the realities of life had returned. Once again, I was cleaning up puke now with staples in my stomach. I cried again.

We were able to bring Casey home the next day. She was colicky for the next two months and never slept more than two hours at a time. I was so tired I could barely function. I was so stressed that milk production was not good, and she wasn't getting enough to eat. She was always hungry. Against the advice of all books and the doctor, I started giving her a spoonful of rice cereal mixed in formula, making the nipple larger so the cereal could get through. It was an immediate drug! The first time she slept four hours, I thought she had died. But she survived and thrived from then on!

The burden of going back to work, trying to take care of a newborn and a sick husband weighed heavily. My husband's rare two to three days of feeling decent provided little relief. He needed his rest. When he was home from the hospital, he spent hours playing "thumper" with the baby on the couch. He talked to her nonstop, and she would thump her legs against the couch in response. It thrilled him. When she grew bored with that, he would play "foreheader" with her.

As he touched each part of her face, he chanted over and over again, "Foreheader…eye see-er…nose smell-er…mouth chopper…cheek tweaker…ear hear-er." He loved spending time with her until she spit up on him. That would make him nauseous, and he, in turn, would have to throw up.

*****

We were very hopeful that my husband would recover and beat the cancer. We were counting on that 70 percent survival rate. The cancer count in his blood went from thousands down to seven. The doctors were hopeful they could get it to zero and operate on the tumors. The surgery was scheduled in hopes that the goal would be reached soon. But he developed a cough, and the cough worsened very quickly. The doctor took X-rays and lung biopsies. The biopsies came back negative, but the doctors were not convinced the biopsy tissue had been extracted from the exact dark spots on the X-ray. Nevertheless, they treated him with intravenous antibiotics for a week as if treating pneumonia.

The second set of X-rays was taken after several days, and the lung spots had increased dramatically. The oncologist beckoned me and his parents into a separate conference room where he informed us that the cancer had spread to the lungs, and my husband had less than two months to live. For a moment, you could have heard a pin drop. We were all floored! Here we thought he was at the end stages of chemotherapy and on the road to surgery and getting well only to find out he was at the end stages.

My father-in-law just couldn't handle the news. He stood up, leaned over the table, and yelled at the doctor, "You're wrong! You don't know what you're doing! I want new doctors. You're just incompetent. The biopsies were negative! He has pneumonia!"

The doctor very calmly looked him in the eye and replied, "You can get all the second opinions you want…the cancer has spread so much that I don't need to take biopsies. I can reach down his throat and pull out cancerous tissue at this point!" I don't know if the doctor was exaggerating or not, but the picture was vivid. I just cried.

My husband's parents, understandably, were having a very difficult time accepting the diagnosis. They researched all sorts of alternative treatments and finally decided they wanted to send him to Greece for a month for experimental treatments. The treatments were very expensive, and they were very angry with me when I informed them that not only could I not pay for the treatments, but I could not take off work to go to Greece. I had to work in order not to lose my job. I just couldn't take off a month at that time to go chasing an experimental treatment that was not covered by insurance.

I expressed my desire to keep him home so that he could spend time with Casey. But within ten days, he was on an airplane to Greece with his mom. When he returned home weeks later, he was in a wheelchair and frail. His hair had grown back out, and he was so handsome. They had declared him cured in Greece and said he just needed to regain his strength. Within two weeks, he went into respiratory failure.

He had been staying at his parent's house so they could look after him and help him regain his strength. I was at work all day and then left for the long drive to pick up Casey, not getting home until after 6:30 p.m. He died the first time on my birthday. I wasn't with him at the time. My friends had taken Casey and I out to dinner for my birthday just to get me out of the house. That evening, my husband went into respiratory failure while at his parent's house. The emergency technicians revived him and rushed him via helicopter to the emergency room where they put him on a respirator for his remaining time. I didn't find out until I got home and heard the message on the answering machine from my in-laws. The guilt of not being there haunted me for years. Sometimes I still dream of the Darth Vader sounds that I never grew used to during the last weeks of his life.

*****

Casey was five months old when her dad passed away from the cancer. I would often wish Casey could remember him playing with her or remember the way he would gaze at her and talk to her as if she could understand every word he was saying. He was so proud to be a dad, especially of Casey. Like most dads, he thought her to be an extraordinary child...and I too believed she was. She certainly had a personality and always knew exactly when to coo and smile, although there were many times, I'm sure it was just gas!

From then on, it was the two of us. She was my life, the bright spot in every day. At about six months old, she became so much more animated. Every day became a new adventure. Rather than a lump of flesh that I coddled each day, she began to sit up and take interest in the world and the people around her. She seemed to always have a pleasant attitude and rarely cried unless she was sick, hungry, or tired. She was a ham for the camera and seemed to have a knack for being perfect in photographs...and she still does!

The "village" who raised my daughter were such special people. Nana Leta, her godmother, kept her each day for the first year and a half while I worked. It was worth the twenty-four-mile drive to know she was with her. Leta had been like a surrogate mother to me for years. She knew the good, the bad, and the ugly...and yet she still loved me, shared God's love with me, and spent hours of her time discipling me in God's word. She taught me what it was like to pour one's life into another person. I trusted her with my life as I had trusted no one before!

One day, I received a call at work from Nana, asking me to meet her at the emergency room. I was in a state of panic. Casey had fallen off Nana's countertop in the kitchen. As far as we knew at that time, Casey was still unable to get out of her carrier. But when Nana went into the other room to put laundry in the drier, Casey wriggled out of her carrier, rolled herself along the counter, and proceeded to fall to the floor, head first. Nana rushed her to the hospital, and after running several tests, they assured us there was no damage. There was not a scratch or a bruise...just a red mark on her onion head to match the bright tuft of hair on top. I always told Nana that if Casey turned out stupid, it was because she had dropped her on her head.

Nana always told me that it was good she fell on her head because she was such a hardheaded kid!

Other than that, Casey went along unscathed for the most part in her first year of life. She had several ear infections, colds, and one bout of croup that scared the wits out of me. It reminded me of the Darth Vader sound. I called Nana at 1:05 a.m. to ask what I should do. She was always so patient with me. Following Nana's directions, Casey and I went into the bathroom, shut the door, got undressed, and stood in the shower, letting the hot water steam up for the next half hour until the hot water ran out. I felt like a prune, but Darth had left.

Casey was famous for spitting up and was an equal-opportunity spitter-upper. It didn't matter who it was, although certain people felt especially targeted. Each time Grandpa Colvin would hold her, she would spit up on him. He would go change his shirt, thinking he was safe, and she'd promptly spit up on him again. He really thought she had it out for him, but actually, she just spit up all the time. She loved to swing in her windup swing. She would sit there for hours and hours perfectly content. About every half hour or so, she would spit up all over the floor. There were so many stains on the carpet in that area that I finally had to move the piano over the stains when she outgrew her swing.

*****

But the disastrous year seemed to drag on. Several months after my husband died, bill collectors started calling me about his hospital bills. I couldn't figure out what was happening. The deductible had been met, all out of pocket costs met, all co-pays paid, and yet there were thousands that seemed to be unaccounted for. I called the insurance company to find out the problem. They politely told me, "All claims have been paid. We've been sending the checks to your new residence rather than the provider after you called to tell us you had moved. The notes say you stated that you had paid the claims yourself, and you were requesting that all checks be sent to you at the new address."

I promptly informed her that I had not moved, had not called, and had not received any checks. She let me know that all checks had been cashed with my signature on the back. When I asked what address she had been sending the checks to, I found that it was the address of my in-laws. I was devastated.

There were tough decisions to be made. The insurance company informed me the only way to recoup the money was to file suit against my in-laws. Then they could prosecute and reissue the checks if they were found guilty. They informed me as well that if found guilty, there would be mandatory jail time. I was so angry. How could they do this to me? To us? How could I forgive them? How could I learn to love them again? How could I afford to pay the medical bills? But how could I put my child's grandparents in jail?

I prayed for days and days. The only answer I seemed to get was "be obedient." That's not an easy answer. God tells us to love even our enemies, even those who have wronged us, but I didn't *feel* like loving them. I didn't even like them at that moment. When I confronted them, they admitted to it and cried. They explained that they were trying to cover the debt they got into for the trip to Greece.

I wasn't sure I could get through the anger and betrayal, but Nana Leta wisely gave me this advice, "It doesn't matter what you feel like...just be obedient, act in love, and God will bring the feelings along later."

And that's exactly what happened. Every two weeks, I took Casey to see them. I was kind and thoughtful, remembering them on all holidays. I made plans with the providers to pay a little each month. It took me years to pay those bills, but God was faithful. And within the next year, I truly came to love my in-laws again. It was a valuable lesson in learning how faithful God is to honor obedience in our live. It was also an unforgettable reminder that God constantly forgives me when I hurt him, yet he is merciful, faithful in his grace and forgiveness, even when I am undeserving. It was a valuable lesson in learning a bit more in the area of "it's not about me!"

*****

My mother died within a year of my husband. Not only was I a widow, but I was now officially an orphan. I don't care how old you are when your parents die, you still feel like an orphan. I was so sad. It had only been a couple of years since we had reconciled. Our relationship was getting so much better. She was still an addict. But as I had grown up, God had mercifully developed compassion in me. Addiction is such a horrible thing. I wish I could have understood it better while she was alive. There are so many regrets. I just didn't know how to handle all the situations.

It seemed she always called me before her suicide attempts. I would answer the phone, and breathlessly she would say, "I just wanted to say goodbye." And then she would hang up.

Invariably, I would get on a plane to go rescue her. The last time it happened was a few years prior to her death. She was living in San Antonio, and I in Chicago. I rushed to the airport, bought a last-minute ticket at an exorbitant price and flew out right away. I took a cab to her apartment. When I arrived, I got no response from ringing the doorbell or banging on the door. I felt desperate to do something—anything! I finally decided to break a window and climb in. I shoved my carry on through the window. (They make it seem like it's easier to do in the movies; it took several attempts!) I found her in the bedroom passed out with six empty bottles of Darvocet. Each had been filled the prior day. Her breathing was shallow and pulse thready. I called 911, got directions to the nearest hospital, and proceeded to rouse her as best I could, wrapping her arms around my neck and mostly dragging her to her Cadillac. She had lost so much weight and was so lifeless! I wasn't sure I could wait for an ambulance.

When I arrived at the emergency room, I went in and reported the overdose and had the staff come to the car to get her. I was so angry and scared; I dumped her there and left. I had to get away to calm down. I felt like my heart was going to beat out of my chest.

I went by the hospital later to check on her. The nurses told me they had pumped her stomach. She had been admitted and was still unconscious. I went back to the apartment with the broken window in a city I didn't know and cried myself to sleep.

The next morning, I went to the hospital to see her, not quite sure how I was going to respond or what I was going to say. When I walked into the room, Momma was awake and sitting up. She looked at me and asked, "Why did you have to embarrass me like that?"

Rockets exploded in my head. As deadpan as possible, I looked her in the eye and replied, "It's over…this is the last time I'm going to rescue you. Next time, you can just die. I'm not coming again if you pull any more of these stunts. I'm done with it!"

I turned and walked out of the room and headed back to Chicago. And as far as I know, she never attempted suicide again.

Chapter 5

By the time Casey was eight months old, we had settled into a routine. Each weekday, I got up early to take her to Nana's. After work, I made the thirty-minute drive to pick Casey up and made the longer journey back home from Nana's. It seemed each week, she was doing something new and exciting. Parenting books indicated that most children start by crawling backward. Not Casey...forward ho! She was crawling around everywhere and pulling herself up by eight months.

The first solid food Casey ate was a plum. After work, one evening, I went to pick her up at Nana's. Papa, her godfather, was sitting at the kitchen counter, holding her in his lap, with a plum stuck to her face. When I walked in, he was laughing hysterically. "Look at this," he said. He would pull the plum away from her face, and she would scrunch her face up and scream bloody murder. He'd put it back in her mouth, and she immediately silenced. It acted as a pacifier. Gumming at it ferociously, she would attack it with her whole face. It became a game they would play, but I was the one who had to pay for it later with her diarrhea!

The first year of Casey's life continued to pass quickly. I loved being a parent! Every day was an adventure. At eleven months, she took her first step. I was so excited. My friends and I would sit in the living room on weekends and spend hours making her walk back and forth. Her chubby little legs motoring along were entertainment in itself. When she mastered the walk, she became a climber. Her focus was always on things above her head. Never did I find her eating food off the floor, and she was never curious about electrical outlets.

This child wanted to see what was above her. Because she wasn't tall enough to see what was on top of the dining room table, she would pull the table cloth off to discover what treasures lay above her. She pulled every sheet of paper off my desk to see if there was anything interesting for her to see. She climbed on chairs, got pots from under the sink to stand on, and tried to access things above her any way she could. This stage would last for a while!

We celebrated Casey's first birthday with a green cake since her birthday was on Saint Patrick's Day. By the time the party was over, she was feverish with an oncoming cold, completely green from the icing, as was the table, the carpet around her chair, and her hair. We had made it through the first year! Parts of it seemed to pass by much too quickly, and at other times, the pain and loneliness of losing my husband made life seem to pass by in slow motion.

As a one-year-old, Casey loved to attack dogs and cats with affection. She had no fear. She loved to sit in the garden and eat dirt clods when I wasn't looking. In fact, she loved to eat almost everything except onions and tomatoes. She particularly liked green peas, corn on the cob, and pasta. I'd have to say she wore her spaghetti well! She screamed bloody murder when a piece of corn would get stuck between her few teeth. But with green peas, she was especially talented. She figured out a way to stuff green peas up her nose and spit them out her mouth. I never could figure out how she did that without choking, but she thought herself to be quite clever.

From the time she got her first bottle, she was a "bottle girl." She never wanted a pacifier or her thumb. She would carry her "botu" everywhere and would sleep with an empty bottle clutched to her chest. She never favored a particular stuffed animal or baby doll at this stage, just her botu. When she finally bit the nipple off one day during a nap, I had to take the botu away from her for good to keep her from choking. *That* was extreme trauma for her and me. It took weeks to get through that!

Talking came quickly for my redheaded bundle. Her first word was *see*. Everything was a finger point with see. She was stuck on just that word for a while. It made me think how simple life could be if, indeed, we would all just simply see. There would be no hidden meanings, no innuendos…just seeing, but life never was that simple. The black-and-whiteness of childhood quickly fades into too many grays.

Her second word was *kitty*. I'm not sure how that happened. We didn't have a cat, nor did we have books about cats. I didn't particularly even like cats, so they were not generally part of our conversation. *Mom* came third, and after that, the new words flew into use. As the year progressed, she quickly began to put words together. She learned to run, to pout, to climb even higher, and to manipulate Mom. Each learning experience was an adventure for both of us.

Casey was still sleeping in her crib. She seemed content to lay there in the morning or after nap time and play with her bear mobile if she woke up early. There were many mornings I was awakened by her having a conversation with herself…or singing. I would lie there and listen until she grew bored and cried out to be rescued.

One morning, I woke to hear a muffled "Mommy, Mommy, help!"

It wasn't really a cry; it was more a pleading. I couldn't figure out where the sound was coming from. I went into Casey's room, but she wasn't in her crib. I ran into the other rooms frantically trying to find her. She was nowhere to be found, and my heart was hammering.

Then I heard the muffled pleading again. "Mommy, Mommy, help!"

I stopped, listened closely, and followed the sound back to her bedroom, but I couldn't find her anywhere. Seeing the slightest of openings in the double sliding doors of her closet, I finally shoved them back to find my toddler huddled on the highest shelf. She had climbed out of her crib, down to the floor, and up to the top shelf of the closet, six feet off the ground. Her closet had wire organizers, and she had used those like a jungle gym to get to the top, but she was stuck and couldn't get down.

I looked up at her, and she meekly said, "Casey need help!" That was the day we got rid of the crib and purchased her first bed.

*****

Casey's journey toward becoming a two-year-old continued to pass quickly. As time flew by, I treasured the experiences and tried to capture each moment. I journaled *everything*! Parenthood was the best thing since chocolate! It was entertainment, joy, and a constant state of awe. Even the simple things like running provided great memories. Actually, running was a comedy at first. Casey looked a bit awkward when she ran and would try to go very fast. However, she didn't learn to stop very well. She would go plowing into walls or the sliding glass door. She would just turn around and laugh. She became quite famous for crashes and falls, never crying unless you asked if she was all right. Lesson: If you ignore the boo-boos, you'll know if she is really hurt or not. She'll cry without you asking!

I bought her first tricycle during this year. I was anxious for her to be an athlete. To my dismay, she would walk around and around the tricycle and then finally sit on the seat with her feet firmly planted on the ground. She wanted nothing to do with pedaling. She wouldn't even let me push her on it. She would stubbornly drive her feet into the ground and state no! I suppose I was a little early with the tricycle thing.

The year was also busy. Casey was quite the traveler from the time she was young. When we flew, she was as good as gold. As we entered the airplane, each passenger would avoid eye contact, hoping I would sit somewhere else. When we took our seats, you could see the people around us cringe. It was written all over their faces. "Oh no…a crying child the whole flight." Invariably, by the end of the flight, Casey would have charmed them to pieces, and, of course, she never cried.

There was a trip to Hawaii, where she waded naked in the waves. She loved the ocean and was fond of water in general. She had always liked to take a bath, and now she loved swimming. We purchased a small kiddie pool for the backyard when we returned, and she would stay in the water, slathered with sunscreen, until she was a prune.

However, her love of water and lack of fear around it would get her in trouble at times. Before my mother died that year, I took Casey to North Carolina to visit. It was May, and the weather was warm enough to take Casey for a walk in Reynolda Gardens. We walked along a wooded path that ran beside a stream. She wanted to walk on her own and would have bursts of running thrown in at times, many times resulting in crashes. Being the curious sort, she ambled toward the edge of the stream.

"Stop right there! Do not move!" I yelled out.

But, of course, that was a signal that this was something very exciting to experience. It all felt like slow motion; she stepped closer toward the edge of a small hill that led to the stream, staring up at me with a smile on her face. I watched as she took a step and tumbled into the stream face down and began floating with the current. It was the scare of my life! I raced down the hill, jumped into the stream, and trudged several feet through the cold current to retrieve my child who was, by now, covered with dirt, moss, and sticks. She was drenched through and through, sputtering dirty water. She seemed relatively untraumatized, but I was a basket case! How was I going to explain this to Momma? I stripped her of her wet clothes, but she was still covered in all kinds of debris. I wrapped her shivering naked body in my arms and rushed her home to a welcome towel and Grandma's arms.

My mom loved Casey so very much. It was the one thing I felt I had actually done right! Momma always wanted to do everything for Casey. She bathed her in the kitchen sink; she sang to her at night and nap time; she spent long minutes combing her little tuft of red hair on the very top of her head, putting it in a tiny ponytail.

Momma had remarried a few years back, and Grandpa Colvin was one of Casey's favorite characters. He took her for walks and read to her. Grandpa continually sang, "I love you a bushel and a peck…a bushel and a peck and a hug around the neck."

He must have sung that song a hundred times to her during that visit. Each time he finished, Casey would giggle and say, "More! More!" She captured the hearts of everyone she was around!

Chapter 6

That trip was the last quality time Momma got to spend with Casey…or with me. She died shortly after her fifty-seventh birthday. She had been fighting a resurgence of the cancer again and had received a bad blood transfusion, contracting hepatitis. That was before blood banks screened blood for hepatitis C. Momma seemed at peace toward the end. She said she was ready to go. I think she may have been ready for a while. In those last days, I took the time to ask questions that I had always been afraid to ask or had asked before but seemingly without getting an honest answer. During her times of lucidity, we had some wonderful conversations. I told her about the time I took her new Buick out after church on a Sunday night and hydroplaned into a cornfield. I told her I was so relieved it didn't hurt the car because I knew she would never let me use it again. To my surprise, she informed me she already knew about that event. When she backed the car out to go to work the next morning, there were corn husks all in the driveway. She got out, looked under the car, and found more stuck under the car. She never mentioned it to me. I think she knew a *lot* more than she ever let on. I guess most parents do!

I finally got up the nerve to ask her, once again, why she didn't love me as much as my brother. That was truly the way I saw things. I expected to get the same answer I had received the few other times I had asked.

"I don't love him more…what are you talking about?"

But this time, it was different. She paused, looked away for a moment, and then looked me directly in the eye, stating, "It's not that I love him more…I just love him differently. He needed me, and you never did. You never seemed to need anyone."

I was floored! How could I have hidden all my insecurities so well all those years? I was desperate for people's love, especially hers. But over the years, I had built so many walls that it was difficult to let people in. I didn't want to ever be disappointed or hurt. So I figured if I never let anyone in or close to me, I would have less chance of getting hurt. Funny how it didn't seem to work that way! I knew the Bible said not to swear that you will do this or do that. I had always taken that literally, so I didn't use the phrase, "I swear I'll do this." But I learned that you could swear things in your heart that you don't necessarily voice out loud. I had sworn to myself that I would not let people get close…that I would not let people hurt me…that I would not grow up to be an addict or closed off to my children. Lesson learned: Be careful of what you swear…even in your heart. You tend to become those things! I continue to this day to miss my mother, but I missed her more while she was here.

*****

After leaving for college, I rarely returned home. It wasn't a place that held good memories for me. When I did visit, Momma would usually pass out from overmedicating. When she visited me, I always had to be on my guard. I was afraid that she could and would pass out at any time. Once, I ventured to introduce her to a boyfriend in college. She was an hour away, having gone to a medical checkup at Duke Hospital. We drove over and met her at a very nice restaurant for dinner. Things were going well for the first half hour, but I had warned him about the possibilities.

When Momma excused herself to go to the restroom, I looked at my boyfriend and warned him, "Beware. When she comes back, it may get ugly."

Fifteen minutes after her return, she started to slur her words. Finally, she passed out cold with her head falling in her plate. We had to carry her out and take her to a hotel for the night.

Or there was the time when I was working at one of my first jobs, Momma flew in to see me coach my college team one weekend. It was a playoff, and I was so proud of the success my team had accomplished that year. I picked Momma up from the airport and left her sitting in the stands on the top row. Halfway through, there was a commotion. Momma had passed out and fallen backward. An ambulance had to be called, and they took her away.

There were so many embarrassing times like that. It was sad to recount them all. How she must have suffered. I'm sure there had to have been times when she would promise herself not to take the pills only to have the addiction win out. There would be times I would come home to visit, and the first thing I would do is go through the house to flush pills down the toilet. She made it for about a day. Then she started yelling at me for taking her pills. She suffered through the weekend in a miserable state until I left and then went back to a doctor for more pills. To me, at the time, her anger and withdrawal symptoms were better than her passing out. It took me a very long time to understand that addiction is a terrible disease… one that takes its toll on the whole family. At the time, addiction was beyond my comprehension. I just could not understand!

I continued to miss what might have been. I grew up not really understanding how marriage worked or what a stable family life was like. It took me so long to understand what unconditional love was. It took me so long to learn how to be unselfish. It took me so long to trust and open up. My whole life had been about self-preservation. It was only through the love I had for my child that I learned many of these lessons. The words of 1 John 4:19 became so very real to me in parenthood. "We love because he first loved us." I had no other explanation for how deeply and thoroughly and completely I loved my daughter. How I wish I could have learned those lessons earlier in life! I wanted to have close relationships, but I was so afraid of them at the same time. I never had close friends growing up. Loving and caring seemed to bring rejection and pain.

I had so much to learn when I set out for college…and not just things from books! I had never really dated a lot. I never even had a "birds and bees" talk with my mom. College brought out my naivete in a glaring way. I had no idea how to relate to the male sex. The first time a guy tried to French kiss me, I had no clue what was happening. I panicked and hid my tongue in the back of my mouth, thinking, *Surely, he doesn't want to touch my tongue.* Several months later, I was reading one of my mom's romance novels and read the description of a couple's passionate kiss…about how their tongues intertwined! The light bulb came on! No wonder those guys never asked me for a second date!

I was engaged a few times in my twenties. It became rather embarrassing to think about how many times I had been engaged! First, there was a college football player, who grew up to be a cocaine addict. Then there was a professional hockey player, who never quite made it to the top of his game. Next came a college professor who claimed to be divorced but whose wife called me after he gave me the engagement ring and promptly informed me that he was not divorced. Following that was a business owner who, I later found, was having an affair with a woman who had six children while engaged to me. Then came a bodybuilder who still lived at home. Next, there was another bodybuilder who tried to get into acting. By the time I met Casey's dad, I was pretty jaded and didn't have a lot of trust in the male species. But then again, I didn't trust much of anyone at that time. To be honest, I didn't even trust my own judgement! As I looked back at my relationship decisions, my ability to discern character in a person seemed to be lacking. I regarded my interpersonal skills development as retarded. It seemed I had to learn everything by trial and error…mostly by error!

Chapter 7

Gradually, I became a bit more of a seasoned parent. Rather than make the long drive out to Nana's each day, Casey stayed with a very nice lady, Regina, who already had six children of her own and missed having a baby around the house. Casey loved it there and fit right in with Regina's kids. They played with her, read to her, and treated her just like one of their siblings. Casey thrived in that environment. Her vocabulary and speech patterns improved rapidly, and she had so much fun. I worked at a university as an associate athletic director during this time. So Casey attended almost every kind of sporting event. She was there before the game, during the game, and after the game since I worked most of the games. Her presence was such a staple that the press who covered the games got to know her. They made film clips of her prancing in her university gear, and friends would tell me the next day how they saw her on television. In fact, I think more people in the community knew me as Casey's mom without even knowing my name!

She was a strong, healthy baby who was over the one hundred percentile mark in height, weight, and head size. It always seemed to me that she needed to grow into her head. I hoped that somewhere along the line, she might get a neck! With roly-poly thighs and short legs, I was afraid she would be all out of proportion. But once she reached thirty-six pounds, she held fast and started to grow upward without gaining additional weight. All of a sudden, she had knees and elbows! Her hair was also growing and became a beautiful, curly, strawberry blonde. She was starting to blossom!

This was also the year of the first kiss! Casey was about twenty months old, and we were at the airport, waiting for a recruit's flight.

We were sitting in the lobby area, waiting for additional flight information when a two-year old boy toddled over with his nanny to speak with us.

He walked right over to me and said as clear as a bell, "Your little girl sure is pretty. May I kiss her?"

I replied (as straight faced as I could) that he would have to ask Casey for permission. I was sure she would run. But much to my amazement, when he asked her, she merely nodded her head yes and promptly puckered her lips. He laid one right on those puckered lips and said, "Thank you." He immediately turned right around and walked off. The nanny never said a word! It was awesome!

Life was smoothing out somewhat, and I so enjoyed watching her grow and become her own person. There were a few stressful times such as when I left my razor in the bathtub, and Casey tried to shave her legs. She took a huge hunk out of her shin, and I was so fearful it would leave an awful scar. Then there was the time we were shopping for clothes. She was anxious to walk everywhere with me by then. One minute, she was right there with me. The next, she had vanished. I ran through the area, calling for her, but to no avail. I was panicking and about to go to security when I saw a little foot sticking out from a rack of clothes. She was just sitting there, rubbing material against her cheek.

As I peeked through the clothes rack to find her, she said, "Oh, Mommy…these jammies feel so good!" She loved the feel of rayon! In fact, after that, she would often put my underpants on her head and wear them as a hat around the house because it felt good.

*****

That was also the year when she got attached to her first baby doll. Her grandparents gave her a real-life doll that she named Amy. Baby Amy was the ugliest doll I had ever seen! She had a new navel, a scrunched-up newborn face, and all the explicit body parts. Casey took Baby Amy everywhere with her for years. It never failed to draw a comment from others about how ugly that doll was, but it never seemed to bother Casey. She had already learned to love unconditionally!

Other than Baby Amy, Casey was never one to be too interested in toys. Each Christmas, she received more toys from friends and family than she could ever play with. None held her attention for very long. For the first several years, she was more interested in the wrapping paper and boxes than the presents. So when she got bored or distracted opening presents, I would take the rest away and put them unopened in the closet. They would be kept there until another occasion such as a birthday or Easter. Sometimes I would just save them to give to other children for their birthdays. Or we would take them to the hospital to give to sick children at Christmas. Her favorite toys by far were Baby Amy and the pots and pans in the lower cabinets. She loved to crawl in the larger pots to use as her house or bang on the smaller pots to make music for her audience.

This was not the only musical ability she showed during this second year of life. She loved to bang on the piano or pick at notes with her fingers, singing as she played. I sang and read to her every night. She had memorized many of the songs and would play and sing them to me during the day. One of her favorite things to do each day was turn on the radio and dance to the music. Her love for music would only grow over the years. And it would stimulate a new interest in music for me as well. Little did I know that an old dream would be rekindled, and joy would burst from its notes!

The meaning of doctor also became very real to her during this year. The doctor used to be a fun person to visit for checkups, but the realization of the pain they can inflict sunk in when she was eighteen months old and had to go get her shots. The shots were given to her in the leg. She was so angry and screamed and cried for what seemed like an inordinate period of time. It was one of the most pitiful sights I had ever seen when she limped around the house for three days after getting those shots. It was so sad. And the memory stayed with her for years. She associated pain with that doctor. From then on until she was six, whenever we visited the doctor, he would just walk into the room, and she would start screaming! Needless to say, she was probably not one of his favorite patients. We changed doctors when she was six!

*****

The year flew by, and before you knew it, she was turning two. Casey had three different birthday parties. One was held back east with my brother. From there, we drove to Florida with my brother and his daughter for a trip to Disney World. We stayed with my aunt, and she threw her another birthday party. When we returned home, her paternal grandparents also gave her a birthday party. She was so confused and had developed the expectation that she would get a new party every week! She was understandably not happy when I responded no.

She stood there, thoughtful for a few moments, and looked up at me and asked, "Mommy…am I still two years old after all those parties or am I older now?"

I had heard so much about the "terrible twos," and I was dreading them a bit. But the twos turned out to be pleasant and fun. They weren't terrible at all! It was the age of talking, an insatiable appetite for knowledge, and developing logic. One of the first signs of logic occurred right after she turned two. I picked her up after work from the sitter's house. I was always so excited to see her at the end of the workday. We ran toward each other and hugged.

When I backed away a bit, I said, "Give me a kiss!" But I had forgotten to take the gum out of my mouth prior to picking her up. She had a fixation on gum for a few years, and it was not something I wanted her to have because it always wound up in her hair, on the floor, or smashed into pieces of furniture.

She stood there, staring at my mouth, and I repeated, "Give me a kiss!"

She responded, "Give me some gum!"

I smiled at my folly and knew I'd have to offer her a piece, so I compromised, "Give me a kiss, and I'll give you some gum." But she decided to be stubborn and wanted the gum first.

She refused to give in, so I replied, "Okay…no kiss, then no gum!" She didn't get any gum. And I didn't get a kiss!

It was a chilly spring day, so I put her coat on her before we left to go home. She pouted the whole way home about the gum incident and didn't say a word. When we arrived, she walked inside the house, promptly took her jacket off, and threw it on the floor in anger.

With as much motherly force as I could muster, I ordered her, "Pick up your jacket and take it to your room right now!"

She stood there defiantly with her hands on her hips, looked up at me, and responded with reason and authority, "No gum, no jackie!" I couldn't help but laugh! I knew I was in for trouble from then on.

She seemed to become interested in everything that year. I found her curiosity humorous and not at all tedious. Although her behavior did not display the dreaded "terrible twos" as expected, she did, at times, display her Irish temper, throwing herself on the floor to flail her arms and legs, but that behavior only lasted about three weeks. Time-out was introduced, and she responded well…for a while. When she threw a tantrum, she was sent to time-out, which was a small chair in her room that faced the corner. Casey was a very social child, so she did *not* enjoy being in time-out at all in her early twos. After three weeks, she decided (most of the time) that the tantrums were not worth time out.

Time-out threats worked well until the late twos. At that point, when she did something wrong before I could even place her in time-out, she would look at me defiantly and state, "I'm going to sit in time-out…leave me alone." So time-out became an occasional discipline. It was now time to break out the dreaded spanking. I had resolved early on in parenthood not to spank since my spanking experience had been so traumatizing. But after much mental debate, I decided to take James Dobson's advice and spank only in times of willful defiance. The spanking would not be pleasant, and it would not injure her. The spanking would only be given in discipline, not anger. And I promised myself I would always be completely under control. When I finally had to use the spanking technique on her, I truly understood the phrase, "This hurts me more than it does you."

It didn't take Casey long to figure out that if I threatened to spank her and if she continued to act out, I most certainly would follow through with the threat. So she was actually a well-behaved two-year-old and became quite helpful. She picked up her room and unloaded the silverware from the dishwasher. As a special treat, she would clean in between my toes—yes, you read that correctly! Our favorite pastime was making brownies. I would put the ingredients in the bowl, and Casey would stir. Each time I turned away, she would eat a spoonful of batter.

I asked, "Did you eat any of that batter?"

And she would respond with chocolate smeared across her mouth, "No, Mommy...of course not." I no longer had any doubt that sin is inherent...not learned in us humans! I never had to teach my child to tell a lie!

Her interests continued to expand during the year. She became enthralled with music boxes and stuffed animals (especially monkeys) and wanted to collect them. Her room was a zoo! Her spring-loaded rocking horse took the place of her baby swing, and she would take Baby Amy for rides. And as the year progressed, the phone became a fixation. Casey loved to talk to anyone, especially to her friend Jenna. But if she couldn't find someone to talk to, it was not unusual to find her talking to the operator! That was, of course, when you could dial the operator and talk with someone.

Singing became one of her favorite car activities. This was the year I began singing and touring with a contemporary Christian trio. Casey would come to most practices, and we would listen to tapes of the songs in the car for hours as I practiced singing. Before long, she had learned all the words to all the songs and would sing along. After a concert, she was the first to let me know she knew I had messed up the words in a particular song!

During that second year, it became time for potty training. I was never really anxious for her to get out of diapers since I didn't mind changing them, but she became very interested in the potty at about twenty-eight months. She had decided she wanted to wear big-girl panties. So we went out to buy Minnie Mouse panties. She knew she was not allowed to wear them until she learned to use the potty. She would get them out of her drawer and lay them on the floor to stare at them. She finally made up her mind that she was really ready to do this, but there was a small problem with bowel movements. For some reason, that process of eliminating feces was a more difficult concept than urinating. She felt like she was losing part of her body when she went "stinky." Each time she would sit on the potty to go stinky, she would cry, thinking she was losing part of her insides. That stage lasted about two weeks! She took to potty training like a pro after that.

The most frustrating stage of the twos was the "I want to get naked!" stage. We could be anywhere, the tennis courts, the grocery store, rehearsal, church, people's houses; it didn't matter. As soon as no one was looking, she'd whip her clothes off and prance around for the world to see in only her "birthday suit." It created many an embarrassing moment for me. One Sunday morning, the choir was singing a special in church. Casey escaped from Sunday school, went to the anteroom where all the choir members kept their purses and belongings, got into the piano player's purse, put on red lipstick that went everywhere on her face, took her clothes off, and pranced out in front of about nine hundred people while we were singing. I was mortified. I thought if I pretended she wasn't mine, it would all go away. Nana came to the rescue and stepped up to retrieve her. I just wanted to crawl in a hole. Who would have thought she'd actually grow up to be rather modest? At that time, I was sure she'd be an exhibitionist or, at least, a pole dancer!

For the most part, Casey continued to be a well-traveled and well-behaved child. We visited Grandpa Colvin in Philadelphia where he took Casey to the zoo for the first time. I'm not sure who had more fun! She traveled with me to Flagstaff, Arizona, for work that year, and we met up with my brother who was going to help take care of her while I went to meetings. Unbeknownst to me, until years later, my brother took her with him to the Grand Canyon one of the days I was working. He asked someone to dangle her out over the canyon while he took a picture. Years later, he showed me the picture and thought it was quite funny that she would be hanging over the edge! She, of course, was laughing in the picture despite the risk… perhaps an indication of the risk-taker she would become.

Christmas that year took on a new meaning. It was a white Christmas. In fact, it snowed a lot that winter, and Casey loved the snow. She went out and played in it until her face and hands were beet red. The reason for Christmas celebration, Jesus, became more real. Each evening before bed, I read Bible stories to her and prayed. I had been doing that since she was a year old. Jesus had become a person to her, a friend, a companion, and she began her own conversations with him each day. We talked to Jesus at mealtime, at bedtime, and when Mommy was stressed! It was so fun to watch that relationship progress. Presents took on a bit of a different role as well. She wanted to find a way to give to others without *me* buying things. That year, we took the overflow of stuffed animals in her room to the children's ward at the hospital to give to sick children. Choosing which ones to let go of was difficult for her, but it was also very special.

Right before she turned three, I introduced her to tennis and bats and balls. She loved any kind of ball. I would throw plastic balls to her in the yard, and she would try to hit it with a big plastic red bat, or I would take her to the tennis court with a bucket of balls and throw tennis balls to her, and about every eighth ball (if I threw it perfectly), she would make contact with her junior racket. It was a delight, and I wondered if one day, she might be very coordinated.

Also, about this time, I started taking her to Thumpers, a preschool. I felt she needed more interaction with children her own age since she was an only child. Much to my relief, she was a hit right away. The teachers loved her, and she was well-behaved. The only concern they seemed to have was that she would often let other children push her around or come and take the doll or toy she was playing with at the time away from her. Rather than complain, she would just find something else to play with or ignore them. Her meekness concerned them.

Then one day, I went to pick her up, and the teachers were very excited; she had stuck up for herself. They were talking over each other trying to relay the story. One boy was teasing her and kept pulling her pigtails. Finally, it clicked. She shoved the boy in the chest and said, "No, that's not nice. Now you stop that right now!"

The boy, Jeffrey, became her first boyfriend, and she quickly became a leader in the preschool set! She also became the organizer, but mostly she played with the boys. Several times, I would walk in to pick her up, and she would be playing doctor or house, and all the other occupants were boys. She had many a boy who had a crush on her! That would continue all the way until she reached high school when her favorite lines would become, "Mom…what happened to me? I used to be so cute and popular? No one asks me for dates!"

She still was very cute, but to keep her humble, I told her it must be her personality. After laughing a bit, I would tell her, "You can't fight genetics. You take after your mother. I never had dates in high school either!"

Chapter 8

I really didn't date much in high school. At the time, I felt the lack of interest from the opposite sex was due to coming from a low-income family and a divorced home. I felt I couldn't escape that stigma in that town. But in retrospect, I suppose it could have been my personality or my freckles that prevented young men from requesting, or maybe it was the fact that my brother nicknamed me "Rooster" because of my cowlicks, and everyone pretty much called me that. Not too many guys wanted to date a girl called "Rooster!"

I compensated by being the consummate overachiever as I grew older. Everything was a competition to me, and I wanted to be the best. Looking back, that probably irritated (or maybe even intimidated) a lot of people. I wasn't savvy enough psychologically to figure out how it affected others. I was just trying to survive. The high school years were torture in a way. Perhaps they are for everyone. I didn't have cool clothes or a car or jewelry or nice things. I was gangly with strawberry blonde hair and freckles. I was a jock, incredibly shy and introverted, didn't know how to wear makeup (and had none), and generally had a terrible inferiority complex.

I started high school with a very short haircut and played on the varsity basketball team from the time I was a freshman. My unruly strawberry blonde hair flew out in all directions. I was a very late bloomer as well. I had crushes on so many of my brother's friends. They were all the cool jock guys. I always wanted to be in the backyard, playing tackle football or basketball with him and his friends. Momma would shout out the back door, "Let your sister play."

So he and his friends would huddle together and come up with a plan to get me the football and then knock the wind out of me on the tackle. I took it pretty well and sucked it up most of the time. I had finally had enough when at age fifteen, some of his uncool friends started to tackle me and then grope me in the tackle pile.

My brother loved to play tricks on me, but at the time, it seemed like torture. I grew up during a time when all telephones were landlines. He knew a trick to dial certain numbers, and it would make the phone ring as if someone was calling in. When I was in another room, he would make the phone ring, rush to the phone, and answer it, saying, "No, she's not here." Then he'd hang up. I didn't know until years later that no one was really calling. I think the coffee cup he gave me for my thirty-third birthday described our relationship growing up very well. The coffee cup read, "Whenever I get down and sad and depressed, I think about all those times I used to torture you as a child…and it cheers me right up!" Is it any wonder that I continued to be an angry teenager?

I tried so hard in high school to make friends, but I just couldn't seem to break through the barrier. I tried to be cool, but you can't *try* to be cool! That makes you so uncool!

I started working at age fourteen, as soon as I could get a worker's permit. I worked at one of the few clothing stores in town so that I could actually buy new clothes. I grew my hair longer and even tried to dye it bleach blonde with my cousin, but we turned it orange instead. My mom came home and had a fit. She hurried me off to her hairdresser who stripped it of all colors and dyed it back to strawberry blonde that evening. No one at school knew the difference until the color started to wear off weeks later, and I had this silver sheen around my head.

*****

There wasn't much for teenagers to do in our small town. When I was feeling especially angry, I climbed the Chinaberry tree in the front yard that stood beside the road and beaned passing cars with Chinaberries. But more often, I sat on the front porch swing and just watched the cars go by. I especially enjoyed it during rainstorms. On Sunday nights, my brother and I crossed the street to watch Bonanza in color on the television set that was left playing at the Allis Chalmers store. Yes, a tractor store was across the street from our house…and it sold televisions! We couldn't hear it, but we would stand in awe outside the window and be amazed at all the vivid colors on this new invention called a "color TV."

Most of my social life was built around church functions. I sang in the choir, went to church camp each summer, and attended all the other functions they held for youth. School athletic events made up the remainder of my social calendar—basketball games, football games, softball and baseball games. In the summers, "recreation camp" was held every weekday at the local junior high school. They would set up all sorts of games and activities for the youth, and all the kids in town would attend, even those who were home from college. That was the highlight of the summer—box hockey, basketball, kickball, but mostly ping-pong. I would wait in line patiently at the ping-pong tables for my turn. It was "King of the Table," whoever won, got to keep playing. The only people who could beat me were a couple of my brother's friends. And, of course, I had crushes on them. Otherwise, I was King of the Table!

The only other social fun was riding around town on a Friday or Saturday night and then sitting at the Dairy Queen or the Texaco station. But that required a car. My brother was always out being cool with his friends, usually using the only car we had in the family. There were lines of traffic going up and down the streets from the Texaco station to the Dairy Queen and back. I was usually at home on those nights unless my older cousin didn't have a date.

Momma was dating a colonel in the army at that time who drove an old army green Volkswagen Beetle. My brother was out of town in his first year of college on a baseball scholarship. Momma and the colonel often took her car and went to the beach for the weekend, leaving me at home alone. One weekend, I found the hidden keys to the Volkswagen and decided to take it out for a spin on a Friday night. I was feeling very mysterious as no one knew who I was in this unknown car. I would pass by, and people would stare.

I was quite enjoying myself! In fact, I was enjoying myself a little too much, so much so that I ran into the back of another car. I was terrified. My first thought was that the car was going to explode. (I had seen way too much TV!) I had crunched the front end of the colonel's Beetle. It was completely smashed. I got out and ran down the street, fearing the expected explosion. Other cars stopped. It was so humiliating! But mostly, I feared the colonel was going to kill me! The car didn't explode, and I was able to drive it home. It was torture waiting for them to come home until Sunday night. I took a verbal beating, but I survived. However, he never left the keys again where I could find them.

I was actually glad (and incredibly proud) when my brother went to college. I thought I would get the car more often, but it never seemed to work that way. Momma didn't seem to be home much for me to borrow the car. My brother had been away for several months during his first year of college. He really couldn't afford to come home. I had not seen him since summer. I was walking home from school and stopped by the usual drugstore hangout. All the cool kids hung out at the other two drugstores across the street that were next door to each other. All the uncool kids, like me, went to the drug-store on the opposite side of the street. So I was just hanging out, drinking my orangeade when I noticed this handsome long-haired boy outside the drugstore across the street, surrounded by people. His hair was in the new style of the Beatles, and I couldn't stop staring at him. I decided to cross the street to get a better view, and as I was crossing, I was mortified...it was my brother! Sick!

My brother dropped out of school soon after that for a while. He would later go back and be very successful. But for a few years, he hung out at home, and he was the one who got to drive the car again. He grew his hair down to his waist, and the whole town thought he was a druggie. I was even beginning to wonder about him myself. It was freezing cold one night, and I woke up to him on the front porch in his underwear, yelling for Barky. Yes, he had named his dog Barky! I got out of bed, went to the front door, and watched him screaming for the dog, waking up neighbors. I stood there in my nightgown, giggling…Barky was right beside me inside the house at the glass storm door, whining.

The one thing I'd have to say about Momma during our teen-age years was that she would always come to our defense, if necessary. We seemed to rarely need it, but when those times occurred, she was *not* to be messed with. During one of my basketball games, an oppos-ing player tackled me on a breakaway layup. I was knocked silly for a few minutes and laid on the floor in a daze. When the fuzz wore off, I looked around to find my mother on the court in her heels and pencil straight skirt, hitting the other player with her purse. But they didn't kick her out. They just escorted her back to her seat, and the game went on.

One night, my brother took Momma's brand-new Buick out for a Saturday night spin around town. We were awakened late that evening by a phone call from my brother. He was calling from a pay phone at the Texaco station where he had been parked, hang-ing out with some friends, watching the traffic go by. The police in our small conservative town were convinced my brother had drugs. They came and tore Momma's car apart but didn't find any drugs or alcohol. The seats had been taken out and were on the pavement. All the compartments were open, the trunk torn apart, and Momma was fit to be tied. Not only had they torn it apart, but they left it sitting there torn apart. Momma walked the few blocks down to the Texaco station in the middle of night. Seeing the mess, she immedi-ately marched down the street to the police department and, in no uncertain terms, informed them that she was suing them. It was one of the few times I ever saw her really, really angry. The police never bothered my brother much after that. But still, I rarely got the car after that and had to resort back to my trusty bicycle. So uncool!

Chapter 9

Casey got her first real bicycle when she was three years old. Her grandparents gave it to her for her birthday that year. It was pink with training wheels and horsehair on the handlebars. I threw her a big pizza party with cake and ice cream. Birthday parties were important for me…probably because I never really had one. Once again, she got far too many presents. But her favorite was by far the bike. I treated several crash wounds during the ensuing months until she learned to use the brakes…and it took months! She also got her first pair of roller skates that birthday, but we both decided they were far too dangerous. I had purchased my own pair of roller skates, hoping to skate with her, but I wound up skating along behind her as she rode her bike. That arrangement worked fine and dandy until finally, one day, she got the hang of using her brakes. She was pedaling at breakneck speed, and I was trying to catch up to her. Suddenly, she threw on the brakes. I went flying over the top of her, knocking her off the bike and skinning my knee worse than I had since I was twelve years old. Casey got a few scrapes as well, but I, for sure, got the worst end of that fiasco! Never again would I skate behind her.

Soon after she turned three, I started noticing some insecurity in her. My job required me to travel a lot. Casey would usually stay with Nana and Papa when I traveled. One day, I was once again getting ready for a trip, and we were packing to go to Nana's. I had to be out of town for two days, and Casey looked up at me with her big blue eyes as tears brimmed over and said, "When are you coming home *this* time, Mommy? I just want to be with you."

It broke my heart and reminded me of how I felt when I was a child. It was an instantaneous decision for me…like jumping off a cliff. I replied, "This will be the last time. Mommy is going to be home with you after this."

I made the decision that quickly to quit my job. I had no idea how I was going to support us. There had been no life insurance money when my husband died, and I was still paying off the hospital bills that were a result of the insurance fraud, but I knew that I could not let someone else raise my child. I wanted to be there to love her and grow with her, even if we didn't have a lot. She would only be young once, and I was the only parent she had!

I prayed about it throughout the trip, and when I returned, I went in to see my boss and resigned. I'll never forget the look on his face. He said, "You can't do that…you have a child to raise! You're a single parent! How will you support the two of you?"

I answered with a calmness that took even me by surprise, "I don't know exactly, but I know it is the right thing to do. I know I need to be home to raise my child. And I know somehow, someway, God will take care of us and provide."

He shook his head slowly and must have thought I was crazy. There was a freedom in jumping off that cliff. There was something in my heart of hearts that knew God would be there to catch me. And he was!

I put in my two weeks' notice. Each night, I was on my knees, begging God for guidance and protection. Two weeks after I quit my job, I received a check in the mail that included my regular pay for the last month I worked plus a whole year's salary. I was floored! I don't know exactly how my boss managed to do that, but I was so grateful! To supplement Social Security benefits, I piecemealed part-time jobs. They were some of the best years of my life! I taught college biology courses at the community college, substitute taught in the public schools, learned to do medical billing, and to my heart's delight…God opened the door for a new music ministry to begin!

For the first few years after my husband's death, I would sit at the piano each night and write songs. It was like a balm to my soul. I was involved in a Bible study small group through my church and would discuss my hobby with them. They suggested I try to start my own music ministry. All of us began to pray about it, and God opened the door with two other amazingly talented musicians who were also part of my church. A music ministry was born! For twelve years, God allowed me to do my heart's desire. It had always been a dream of mine to sing and write songs. God has an interesting way of bringing circumstances about that lead us to our dreams. It was twelve of the best years of my life! The Bible study small group set up our first concert, raised the money, and funded our first recording project. The ministry took off from there with a wonderful friend agreeing to be the booking agent for a small fee. Casey went with us to almost all the concerts. It became a family affair, and she continued to be quite the traveler.

It was also about this time that Casey also began to pose questions about her dad. Who was he? What was he like? Did he love me? Did he want me? Did he like to play with me? Did he have friends? Was he in heaven? Could he still love her in heaven? Could he still see her from heaven even if she couldn't see him? Did he miss her? I tried to answer each one honestly and tell her everything I could. I'm not sure how much she comprehended or remembered. She seemed to ask the same questions week after week. Perhaps she just needed to be reassured. Mostly, she was just aware that he got sick and died and went to live with Jesus in heaven. At bedtime prayers, she talked with me about him on a regular basis. Over and over again, she would ask me to tell her all the things he used to do with her as a baby. And I did. I told her that he rocked her for hours, sang to her, talked to her, and that he adored her. She never tired of hearing those stories.

In fact, she became a "story girl." I couldn't get her to bed at night or nap time without reading or telling her a story. It was a ritual for us. She loved books and wanted me to read the same ones over and over again. Each night, we would read a Bible story and then a children's picture book. She had a special knack for memorizing books. It was not unusual after reading a book several times to find her in her room or in the front yard "reading the book" to Baby Amy. If she couldn't remember the words exactly, she made up words to match the pictures. She told her own version of the story until she memorized the book. She often read to "her babies." Surrounded by her baby dolls in the double-wide swing out in the front yard, she would rock and "read" her books out loud. Baby Amy always got the prominent place on her right side!

One day, my neighbor knocked on the screen door and asked me to come outside. She whispered, "How did you teach Casey to read at so young an age?" She had stood behind her and had followed her reading the story to the baby dolls, word for word. I just laughed. I'm not sure she actually believed me when I told her Casey had memorized all those books!

We didn't watch a lot of television in those days. There seemed to be so much else to do to occupy our time. But each morning, Casey woke up to watch *Sesame Street*. She also loved to watch movies and would watch her favorites literally a hundred times or more. She could also memorize most of a movie. She watched *ET*, *Little Mermaid*, *Lion King*, *Sleeping Beauty*, *Lady and the Tramp*, *Land Before Time*, *Bambi*, and others so many times it became normal for me to find her parked in front of the television, reciting the dialogue of the film word for word with the characters as the movie went along. It was an incredible thing to watch. She was playing every role!

I tried to be careful what she watched on television, but I came home one night from a concert and found the babysitter had brought the movie *Batman* with her (which became one of her favorites). I was a little upset, thinking it was probably too violent for her. *Shoot...* Jack Nicholson gave *me* nightmares as Joker! I voiced my concern, and Casey looked up at me with this exasperated look, stating, "But, Mommy...it's not *real*." I picked and chose my battles each week, and this one was not at the top of the list that night!

*****

Age three was much more trying than age two, but nonetheless, it was perhaps an even more entertaining year. As her vocabulary and reasoning improved, our conversations grew livelier. Much to my chagrin, she also repeated her first curse word that she had heard from a playmate. Yet I so enjoyed our times together talking. I had always heard "kids will say the darndest things!" And now I knew it to be true firsthand.

More than once at the grocery store, we were standing in line, and she would blurt out loudly, "Mommy, that man's pretty cute...I think he'd make a good daddy!" Or "Hey, Mommy, look at that guy. He has no hair on his head!"

Or there was the time my friends tried to set me up with a date. They invited Casey and I over to their house for dinner to meet the guy. He had a receding forehead, and I was mortified that Casey would blurt out, "Look, Mom, he's bald!" We made it through introductions, and I thought I was safe, but she kept staring at his baggy Jammer pants. (Yes, it was 1990!) Finally, she looked up at him in the awkward silence and stated, "You look like a clown! I think you're quite funny-looking." Needless to say, that guy never did call me.

One particular memory stood out that year of a day when we were waiting patiently to see the insurance man. Two receptionists and seven other people were seated in the waiting room. It was very quiet in the room with most people quietly reading magazines. And it was summer, so I had on shorts. Casey was sitting with me in a large wing chair, rubbing her hand absentmindedly back and forth along my thigh as she studied her surroundings. In the quiet of the room, Casey looked up at me and spoke in her normal loud voice, "Mommy, you have beautiful hair."

I replied, "Well, thank you!"

And she continued, "On your legs!"

Everyone in the room howled. You see, I had never seen the need to shave above my knee, so hair grew freely. And I was quite hairy. But it was blond hair that was not very noticeable at all...to me! I blushed four shades of deep red, but then again, I got used to blushing a lot that year! And I did start shaving my upper thighs!

Most of the time, to my relief, our "entertaining talks" were just between the two of us. They were often quite memorable during that year. Her imagination was a wild and wonderful ride. I never quite knew what would come out of that mouth. One evening, when we arrived home, I took her seat belt off and got her out of the car seat. She started screaming and crying hysterically.

"What? What's wrong?" I asked.

She tearfully replied, "I didn't want you to take off my guitar!"

*****

A consistent topic of conversation was about me having another baby. She often said, "Mommy, I think you need to have another baby."

I would reply, "Oh you do, do you? Should we have a boy or a girl?"

She would consistently answer, "A girl...I want sisters, no brothers."

We had that same conversation numerous times. So one day, I decided to expand the conversation, saying, "And what should we name this baby girl if we get one?"

Without hesitation, she replied, "Larry!" Okay then!

There were so many firsts during that third year. It was exciting. She had her first imaginary friend, Eric, to whom she consistently talked. I never could find out much about Eric, but he was a fixture throughout the year. She got her first pets. She started dance classes and swim classes, and she found the love of her life...gymnastics. We were on vacation in Tahoe with a girlfriend of mine who was also a single parent of two children slightly older than Casey. It was a great condo with a pool and play area for the kids and tennis courts for us adults. We arrived in Tahoe at night, and the next morning, I was downstairs making breakfast. I knew Casey was up and about, but I wasn't hearing a peep from her. As a parent, it made me nervous when a long period of time went by without a sound from my three-year-old. I decided I needed to go look for her and found her parked in front of the television set, mesmerized by the gymnasts who were competing at that time in the Olympics.

She looked up at me very seriously and said, "Mommy, I'm going to be one of them!"

I replied, "Okay, now come eat breakfast."

But she wouldn't budge. Each day, she stationed herself on the couch and wouldn't move until the gymnastics portion was over.

When we returned home a week later, I was hoping she had forgotten. But each day, she diligently asked me if I had signed her up yet for gymnastics. After a week, I finally did...and that began a lifelong love affair with the sport.

At the age of three, Casey was obsessed not only with gymnastics but with her reflection in the mirror, with wearing dresses and bathing suits and with dancing. She occupied herself for hours by putting on a bathing suit and dancing to tapes of music in front of the mirror. She went to gymnastics twice a week. When she wasn't at gymnastics, she was practicing gymnastics at home or thinking about when she could go back.

But at least these new obsessions got her out of the habit of crying when we went to the park and left the swings to come home. She would wail for fifteen minutes and often cry herself to sleep on the way home. I could now tell her we had to go home to practice gymnastics! Joy abounded!

That year for Easter, a friend of mine gave her a couple of real live bunnies. She named them Barney and Lester. We put them on the deck outside for the night in a giant box with a lid. But when we went out to check on them in the morning, they had somehow escaped. Lester was later seen crawling under the deck, and Barney was seen running in the yard, but we couldn't catch them. We continued to put food out each night for about a month. After that, the food didn't seem to be touched. I thought something had eaten the bunnies.

But Casey handled the loss pretty well. Each night, she prayed that God would take care of the bunnies. Then she prayed for a new daddy. She never seemed to get too discouraged at that age. One night, she surprised me by adding to the prayer, "And, oh yeah, God...can you please be making me a husband for when I grow up?" Little did she know that I too had prayed that same prayer each and every night since the day she was born.

The "threes" were definitely a challenging time! It seemed as though each day, my three-year-old tested where the line would be drawn. As a single parent, there were so many times I grew weary of constantly keeping that line in the same place, yet I think deep down she wanted to be disciplined. She didn't really want the line to move. Even though she argued and became obstinate, she usually got over it quickly.

There was, however, quite a long time during the "terrible threes" when Casey got into the habit of waking up in the middle of the night and would come crawl in my bed. It started to become a regular nightly thing. After several months, I thought it best that we break this habit. So when she crawled in my bed the next time, I promptly took her back to her own bed and sat with her until she fell asleep. She didn't handle this well and cried out, "You don't love me! Why won't you let me sleep with you?"

I went back to my room after rubbing her back until she fell asleep and thought to myself how much I am like that with God. When he takes something away or doesn't give me something I want, I often think he doesn't care or doesn't love me enough. It must break his heart in much the same way it broke my heart when Casey cried out. If only I could keep the perspective that he is doing things for my own good, even though it may not *feel* good at the time. He is giving me a hope and a future. My job is to trust and obey.

*****

That summer, we drove eight hours to Boise to visit our friends, Cathy and Pete, for a week. Casey entertained me the whole way. The conversation took many turns and curves. At one point, she earnestly looked up at me and said, "Mommy, tomorrow I want to ride a pony, then I want to ride on an airplane, then I want to ride a spaceship."

Amazing how little minds work. In between our "serious" conversations during the drive, Casey learned to blow her first bubble, and she learned to paint our nails. We had fingernail polish from our knuckles to the tips of our fingers. I was so happy to arrive after that eight-hour trip. Cathy helped me give Casey her bath that night, and when she got out of the tub, she nakedly preened with her hair down to her waist, saying, "Aren't I pretty? Don't I have pretty hair?"

I kept telling her, "Pretty is as pretty does!" That's what my grandmother used to tell me. For a moment, I wondered if I had ever possessed the confidence to preen like that when I was little. But very quickly, I answered that one. No, I was never that pretty nor that confident, and I knew it because my brother always let me know!

Instead of riding a spaceship and a pony, we visited the zoo, went out on a boat ride, and swam in a lake. On the road trip back home, we sang and continued our serious conversations. I asked her if she knew who was first in my life. She responded, "Yes, God is."

I asked her if she knew who was second in my life, and she said, "Yes, Jesus is. But, Mommy, who is that holy guy? Is he third?"

Wow! Three years old was way too young to try and explain the Trinity! Instead, we sang some more songs. We gently sang the words to one of the songs, "When the tears well up inside, and I think my heart will break…"

After the song was over, she turned off the tape player and said, "Mommy, what makes a heart break?"

I told her that a heart will break sometimes when it gets very sad or when it gets hurt. She sat quietly for a few minutes and looked back up at me with a big smile, saying, "My heart won't break!" I told her I hoped not, but I knew that was probably a lie.

I supposed it was possible some people might go through life without having their heart broken numerous times. Then there were others of us who seemed to have it broken over and over during a lifetime. Perhaps it was that way for most people. I wished I could protect her from those things that could break her heart, including her own poor decisions that she may make in the future. Instead, in that moment, I strengthened my resolve to train her up in the way she should go so that when she was grown, she would not depart from it. That was my hope.

As for protecting her from a broken heart, I had to leave that to God. I knew as confidently as I knew anything that he has a perfect plan for her. And I knew from experience that if her heart was ever broken, only God could truly heal it. I also knew that he can (and probably will) use that experience for the betterment of her and others. My prayer was that she would always maintain a close relationship with God so that he can see her through all those times when they do occur. Maybe someday I could help her understand that if

I love her as much as I do (which is an awful lot), how much more God's love for her must be! It's difficult to even comprehend!

*****

We continued reading Bible stories each night. The Christmas story was one of her favorites, and we read it over and over again, even when it wasn't Christmas time. We also continued to read other books, but every night, we would end with a Bible story. One morning, as we were getting dressed, I asked her if she could tell me the story of Jesus. I wondered how much of it she was actually picking up from all the stories we had read.

She was excited and said, "Sure I can, Mommy! Jesus had Mary, and Mary had a little lamb, then she asked Jesus into her heart, and then everyone smiled."

I was a bit stunned and blurted out, "Is that all?"

She responded, "Oh…and Jesus got eaten by a big fish, but he's okay now!" So much for comprehension!

But she did pick up on a lot. There were times when I didn't feel well and was edgy or frustrated, I thought I hid those times well. Yet invariably at a prayer time the next day, such as at meals, she said something like, "God is good, God is great, let us thank him for our food and bless it to the health of our bodies…and thank you, God, for not letting my mommy be grouchy today."

I guessed she noticed! It was at those times I asked her forgiveness, and we would kneel and together ask God to forgive me and help me. After the prayer was over, she often looked up at me and said, "Mommy, you're so cute. I'm so glad you're my mommy." Oh, to be able to look at others through the eyes of a child, to be able to forgive that easily, to forget that easily, to love that easily. I had so much to learn!

Chapter 10

By the time Casey was three, I had started dating again and had become quite serious with a man. When I met Ron, he told me he was a divorced father of one and an independent construction contractor. He drove me around, showing me houses and projects he was working on. He was so good to me and was wonderful with Casey. Casey began to ask if that might be "the daddy" God had in mind for us. He was kind, generous, loving, fun, and spent a lot of time with us. I was skittish and nervous but beginning to have hope that I was getting to the point where I could fully trust a man again. He went to church with us, prayed with us, and seemed to enjoy looking out for us. It seemed like the perfect fit. As I began to earnestly pray about it, I felt tremendous reservations but couldn't figure out why. There was just a part of my heart that wouldn't let go fully. When he asked me to marry him, I told him I wanted to say yes, but there was just something in my heart holding me back, and I couldn't figure it out. I relayed to him that I had prayed about it fervently and felt that I was getting a no for an answer. It's one of the few times I can remember him being angry. He seemed to get a bit freaked out and went home abruptly that night.

I thought perhaps I just had cold feet. Ultimately, I let my guard down, and we attended premarriage classes at our church, "graduating" with the blessing of the church. But I still felt uneasy for some reason. I continued to pray, asking God to show me the right thing to do…to open a window very clearly so that I could see. Well, indeed, God did answer that prayer.

I had just come home from work and flipped on the television in the bedroom to catch the six o'clock evening news while I was changing clothes. I heard his name first...then Ron's picture flashed across the screen. He had been arrested for manufacturing and distributing drugs. I was stunned! What scared me to death was that he had picked up Casey for the afternoon. She was supposedly at his house, playing with his daughter for the afternoon. I was panicked; my heart was racing. I just couldn't believe it. How stupid could I be? How naive could I be? How totally unaware and fooled could I be? Most of all, I was angry. I had not felt that kind of anger since I was very young.

I gathered my purse and was headed out the door to who knows where...I couldn't even think straight. I had no idea where I would have driven to. I didn't even know where he was or where my child was at that time. I just knew I had to do *something*! As I walked toward the garage door, the front doorbell rang. I ran to the door, thinking it might be someone with Casey. When I answered the door, two DEA agents were standing there...alone...no Casey. They introduced themselves to me and told me not to panic. They informed me there were agents at Ron's house who were there with him and the two girls. Although they were there to arrest him, the agents had ordered pizza for the girls and were waiting for the moms to pick them up before taking him into custody. I was so grateful. I was also worried they might think I had something to do with this. Before I could state my concern, they also informed me that they had been watching me for the past six months and knew that I was unaware of Ron's activities. They assured me they were aware of my ignorance of his operation. They even apologized profusely for having been unable to warn me beforehand. The sympathetic agents then drove me to Ron's house.

When we arrived, I was so angry I was visibly shaking. The girls were in the kitchen, eating pizza and laughing with one of the DEA agents. Ron was in the other room, crying. I walked up to him, slapped him as hard as I could, and seethed. "How could you have endangered my child this way?"

Then I gathered up Casey and left without saying another word. The agents drove us back home while Casey told me how much fun she had been having, wondering why we had to leave so suddenly. But she didn't ask too many questions. She merely held my hand and tried to comfort me. She had an innate sense that I was not doing well. She always had a special knack for reading my emotions no matter how hard I tried to fake it.

*****

It took me a long time to get over that anger…almost a year. It took me longer than that to finally forgive. It ate me alive. It took years for me to trust my own judgment in people after that. I didn't want to leave the house. I started to have panic attacks when Casey would spend time away from me at preschool or with relatives. Eventually, I started throwing up and couldn't seem to stop for weeks. I ceased answering the phone, and finally one day, I heard someone banging on my door. I looked out the peephole to see Nana standing there with an axe in her hand…seriously an axe!

She started yelling, "I know you're in there…you either open this door or I'm going to chop it down!" I believed her.

I opened the door, and she ordered, "Get dressed…we're going to the doctor." She loaded Casey and I in the car and off we went to the emergency room. Once again, I was angry! But at least I was feeling something other than morbid despair.

"I thought we were going to the doctor," I stated upon arrival at the hospital.

She just ushered me out of the car without a word, carrying Casey. I threw up in the waiting room, mostly with dry heaves. They finally took me back to the examination room, monitored my vitals, and did blood work. It didn't take long for them to admit me. The doctor told me that my liver functions were shutting down, and that my blood had become toxic to my system. He also informed me he would not give me any medication at that time because he did not want to put any more strain on the liver. I didn't really understand much of what was going on at the time. I was so dehydrated and weak.

I remained in the hospital almost three weeks while Casey stayed with Nana. The second day, a psychiatrist walked in my hospital room and, without introducing himself, asked me, "Are you trying to kill yourself?"

Then I was really angry. *That* would be the last thing I would do to my daughter after what happened in *my* childhood. I emphatically told him that fact. He was very stern with me and told me that if I didn't get help, that was exactly what I was going to do to myself. He informed me I had become clinically depressed, and my systems had started to shut down. He could not guarantee that all my liver functions would return to normal. I knew I had been down in the dumps for the past year, but wouldn't anyone be after the circumstances I had been through? How could I have not known how bad I was? Was I that out of touch with myself?

I laid in the hospital day after day, not having much to do but think. I thought of all my mother had gone through, how depressed she must have been, how I was never able to understand it. Finally, I had some inkling of being out of control. Empathy for her seized me, and I wished so much that I could have run to her, hugged her, apologized to her, and told her that finally, I understood…even if just a little. Instead, I just cried at the lost opportunity.

By the end of those three weeks, I was determined to get better. I had a precious gift of a child that I wanted to be there for, to nurture and to take care of. The one thing in the world I wanted to be was a good mother…at all costs.

A year of therapy was good for me. I had never really believed in psychiatrists or therapy. After all, they had not done my mother much good! My skewed belief was that they had all become psychiatrists because they were so messed up to begin with! But it really did help me to talk about all the "pink elephants" that had been sitting on my couch for so long. There were so many things I had never told anyone. I had kept them to myself, thinking them to be far too shameful to ever reveal. For years, I had let shame lord over me. But there was something freeing about sharing those things, even if it was done reluctantly. To have a doctor say, "Okay, so get over it!" allowed me to finally let it go. I learned that most people won't hate me or think me any less of a person because of those things. And if they did, it was their problem! I learned that everyone had skeletons. The one thing I never wanted again was for anyone to pity me in any way. I had experienced enough pity as a child to last a lifetime.

Those events and feelings were not easy to discuss…and nor would they ever be. Sharing them the first time required desperation. Sharing them afterward required trust, and I struggled so much with trust. During one of our first sessions in the hospital, the doctor asked me, "If you had to categorize people as a type of animal, which animal would you choose?"

I thought about the question for a good while. Finally, I responded, "Cats. They're like cats…when they want something, they snuggle up to you. But at other times, they don't want to have anything to do with you. They rarely listen, and you just can't count on them. They're just extremely selfish."

He looked at me with surprise and stated, "Wow! That was well said. I never did like cats!" After that, he and I got along just fine.

The perceived shame of having been so badly broken haunted me for several years. There were times during the years of doing music ministry that I wanted to shout out and declare all my imperfections. Often times, people involved in ministry are put on a pedestal and thought to somehow be a better person than those to whom they are ministering. It was such a lesson in humility for me. I think God allows us broken people the chance to minister because we know the incredible amount of mercy and grace he has shown us. The greater the forgiveness he has imparted, the greater the love the forgiven most likely feels for him. In my case, my love for him was gigantic. I had broken every commandment in the book. Yet his grace had always been truly amazing!

Chapter 11

When I was in college, our family went to Los Angles to the Rose Bowl. I was so excited! We never went anywhere exotic like LA. (When you're from North Carolina, LA seems exotic!) Momma was dating another colonel who was an alumnus of Ohio State, and we were invited to come out for the event. So my brother, Momma, and I set out driving across the country from North Carolina to LA to meet the colonel who had flown out earlier. We took turns driving and sleeping. I had been driving a few hours late in the evening as we arrived in Albuquerque, New Mexico. It was snowing hard, and the roads were treacherous. I had never driven in snow before and was happy that everyone else was asleep when I fishtailed off the road at one point. Perhaps that should have been an omen for the trip.

The Rose Bowl party was at Century City that year. I felt like a movie star as we arrived for the party. (It didn't take much for my imagination to run wild!) I mingled around the large ballroom, eating hors d'oeuvres, listening to music, and thinking I was such a big girl. How incredibly naive I was! I even met a tall handsome young man who told me he was a real estate agent. He was twenty-four years old and wanted to take me around to show me where some of the movie stars lived, including Elvis. When you're young, you can feel wise and invincible. I felt particularly safe because there was another couple going, even though I had just met them. When I asked my mother if I could go, she agreed and wrote down the address of where we were staying so the young man could take me there afterward.

All of us piled in his Mercedes, and off we went. I had never been in a Mercedes! We had only driven a few miles when he stopped and let the other couple out. I was nervous and asked where they were going. He replied, "Oh, they want to be alone."

The other girl looked as nervous as I was but said nothing. I innocently asked if we were still going to look at movie star houses. I'll never forget the look he gave me. He said nothing for a long time…just stared at me with a blank face as he pulled away before saying, "We'll see…we're going to run by my place first."

Then I started to get scared. We drove up to a brownstone unit where he stopped the car. As he started to get out, I just sat in my seat. He looked in and said, "Come on!"

I promptly replied, "I don't think so. I'll just wait here."

Slowly he sat back down in the car and said nothing for what seemed like an eternity. I wasn't sure what to do. I was in a strange city with a strange man with no money in my purse. My mind seemed to be working in slow motion. I remember thinking I should jump out of the car and run as fast as I could. He seemed to be reading my mind. Suddenly, he pulled out a switchblade and popped it open. I had never seen a switchblade either. He held it to my throat and informed me in a cold voice, "You will get out, and you won't make a sound…do you understand?"

He got out of the car again and dragged me unceremoniously across the console of the car. I ripped my nylons, and tears flooded my eyes as my heart pounded. There was no one else in sight. He led me up the stairs and opened the front door with the key. When he turned the light on, the apartment appeared to be sterile and staged. My first thought was, *He couldn't live here! No one lives here.* There were no personal items. There was no lived-in look. He led me upstairs to the bedroom and told me to get undressed. He stood there with the knife pointed at me. Ultimately, he raped me at knifepoint, called a taxi, paid the driver, and gave him the address my mother had written down.

I was so humiliated. I had always been a fighter. If someone had told me that a man would try to rape me, I would have sworn I would fight to my death. Instead, I had been frozen. I couldn't move. I felt like I was in one of those dreams where my feet were lead, and I couldn't run. Tears were running down my face. My nylons were destroyed and had been discarded on the floor of the apartment that was most likely for sale. I felt stupid, cheap, and used. I wasn't even sure at that time if I was grateful to be alive. And I was too humiliated and embarrassed to tell a soul. I never told anyone what happened that night until I talked to that psychiatrist in the hospital many years later. Even after all those years, the tears flowed fresh again, and the humiliation and shame washed over me afresh. Yet in a way, it also seemed to be cleansing to be able to finally tell someone. To my surprise, the doctor didn't see me as shameful. I had always felt it was my fault, and I should have been able to *do* something. One thing was for sure…I would never forget that twenty-four-year-old man's face!

The trip was over soon enough, and I went back to college for the new semester. It was basketball season, and I played for the university team. I was happy to get back to normality and forget about the whole incident. But a couple of months later, I started feeling nauseous. I had missed my period, and the nightmare reared its ugly head again. I was pregnant. I was also mortified. How could this have happened to me? God, why did you allow this to happen? Still, I told no one. It was nearing the end of basketball season, and playoffs were only a month away. How was I going to have a baby? How was I going to tell my family? How would I support a child? How could I love a child from a rape?

I couldn't sleep. I couldn't eat, and when I did, I usually threw up. Abortions had just become legal in North Carolina. Without discussing it with anyone, I went down to the clinic one morning and had the abortion. The procedure seemed so simple and fast. I was out of there that morning in no time. We had a home game that night, and I suited up to play as a starting guard.

I was in a haze during the first five minutes. I scored two baskets…the second on a breakaway layup from a steal. After I made the basket, I thought I was going to black out. I ran to the bench and asked the coach to pull me. As soon as the sub came in, I went to the locker room and passed out on the floor. I woke to the face of the trainer and smelling salts. I told her it was just the flu, that I'd been throwing up and felt weak. She sent me home, and within a couple of days, I felt fine physically.

But the guilt and pain would last for years. For a long time, I wasn't sure if God could ever forgive me. When I finally realized he could and would, I wasn't sure I could ever forgive myself. In fact, forgiving myself was the hardest thing to do. I felt sure my punishment would be that I would never be allowed to have a child in the future. I wasn't sure I could ever trust a man enough to actually get married, much less have a child. It was to be a long road toward learning to love and forgive myself.

Somehow, at thirty-six years of age, with the help of that psychiatrist, I was finally able to come to terms with it and allow God not only to forgive me but to cleanse me of the shame and pain. Finally, I could be free to really love myself and others, including my child, with abandon. I was free to forgive myself, as well as others. But I still didn't trust my ability to discern a good person from a bad person. I couldn't tell the difference between a puppy who wanted merely to love but made mistakes from a wolf who wanted only to hurt and devour.

Chapter 12

The summer when Casey was three, she learned to swim, excelling at "monkey tree rocket ship." As she laid on her back, she curled her hands inward, appearing to tickle her sides like a monkey. Then she extended her arms up and outward like a tree. Finally, she pushed the water down with her arms, acting like a rocket ship, propelling herself through the water. During the last class of the summer, she culminated her lessons by jumping off the high dive, artfully performing a belly flop that scared the wits out of everyone at the pool, especially me. We sat there stunned, waiting to see if she had knocked herself out or if she would come up out of the water. Her little body was beet red, but she didn't cry. She just swam over to me and stated matter-of-factly, "I don't think I want to do that again, Mommy." I wanted to stop and capture the moment. Her little face was so red from splatting the water, and she tried so hard to be brave and not cry. I was so proud of her!

There were so many moments I wanted to capture and freeze in time. Most parents probably feel that way. I wanted her to grow up, but at the same time, I wished I could freeze her at almost every age, especially in some of the more precious moments. Casey would do a lot more belly flops that summer, but they would be off the low dive. She loved the water, and even in the bathtub, she would practice swimming, pushing herself off from the end of the tub, and floating backward.

That summer, she also became fairly proficient at hitting tennis balls. We spent a lot of hours on the court, hitting balls. Each time I played, Casey would tag along and play with other children, hanging out at the courts. After I finished playing, I would hit balls with her. I had big plans for her to become this wonderful tennis player. Gymnastics eventually ruined my grand plan, but it fulfilled hers. As a three-year-old, she had her mind made up...a gymnast she would be!

At the end of that summer, Casey and I had our first real conversation about the difference between the truth and a lie. I had noticed that Casey had started lying to avoid negative consequences, apparently without it bothering her conscience. Although I realized there were sociopaths in this world who don't really possess a conscience, I hoped this was not the case with my child. It was my duty as a parent (along with the Holy Spirit) to instill a sense of right and wrong. What an awesome responsibility for a parent! So much of what a child learns comes from watching you, the parent. I tried to let her know that she would get punished a lot more severely for telling a lie than for telling the truth, even if she had made a bad decision. As time would show, I'm not sure that conversation sunk in and actually meant anything at all to her at the time. This was just another example to me of the innate sinfulness of man: you don't have to teach your child to lie!

The fall brought a series of semi-traumatic events. As we were leaving church one Sunday night, we pulled out of the parking lot, and I stopped to talk to a friend of mine. Casey was playing with a ball in the front seat. (Horror of horrors...that was when most parents put their child in a car seat located in the front seat facing forward.) As I carried on my conversation with my friend, Casey dropped the ball. She adeptly unbuckled her car seat, scooted down to stand on the floorboard, and bent down to pick up the ball. When she stood up, her head hit the windshield and shattered it. She didn't even cry. (I always knew she was hardheaded!) Although it cost three hundred and twenty dollars to repair, I kept telling myself that it wasn't too great a price to pay for no brain damage.

A week later, Casey spent the night with her friend, Breezy. As they laid on the carpet drawing, Breezy rolled over and accidently stabbed Casey in the face with a pencil. The lead broke off in her cheek, and I was sure she would have a permanent "freckle" there the rest of her life. She, however, was very proud of her freckle because it made her more like Mommy.

She also got her first bee sting when picking grapes off a vine that week. When she told me about it, she exclaimed, "I guess I got that bee's grape, Mommy, and he got mad at me!" That bee sting was a topic of conversation for a good two weeks. She would continually tell people to look at her bee sting long after all evidence had faded.

The very next day after the bee sting, we went to the park to spend the afternoon. At that time, Casey was going through a phase where she wanted to go to the bathroom when she got bored with an activity. This habit had become quite a nuisance. I would constantly take her to the bathroom, and it would be obvious she didn't have to go at all. By the time that park day rolled around, she had cried wolf too many times. She told me she had to go to the bathroom, and I didn't believe her. But she showed me, a couple of minutes later, she peed in her pants with the urine running down her legs. I felt so badly! I took her home, washed her up, and told her I was sorry.

That night, I sent her into the bathroom to undress and get ready for her bath. When I walked in, she was standing in the middle of the room, peeing on the floor. I asked her why she did that, and she just looked at me with no response. I asked her again, and again she didn't respond. Then I spanked her and made her help me clean it up. After her bath, I asked her again very calmly, "Casey, why did you pee on the floor?" She was thoughtful for a minute and then responded, "I don't really know why, Mommy…it just felt good. It was all nice and warm going down my leg, just like in the park today." How in the world do you respond to that?

We woke up the next morning and had our Saturday ritual. I would cook pancakes, and Casey would sit on the counter next to the stove. She would stir the batter and talk to me as I got the pan greased and the burner going. That morning, I cooked the pancakes as usual and turned the electric burner off. Once again, as always, I warned her that the burner was hot and told her to stay away from it until I could get her down. As soon as I turned to put the plates on the table, she put her barefoot on the burner, testing the line again. She screamed, I ran over to her, and a big blister promptly appeared

on the bottom of her foot. I tried to explain to h/
her something like that, it was for her own goo/
know my warning was meant to keep her from
to forbid her to do something fun!

She limped around the rest of the day, and as I put her .
I thought how very much we, as adults, are like that. God's word
gives us guidance on what to do and what not to do, but willfully,
we cross the line. How many times have we missed out on God's
best for us because we were not obedient? How many times did we
hurt ourselves testing the line or making decisions to do something
we *thought* would bring us happiness? Too often, people think of
Christianity as a list of dos or don'ts. We sin if we do one of the things
we are not supposed to do on the list or if we don't do one of the
things we *are* supposed to do on the list. But really, sin is just a matter
of the heart. Just as with Casey, we think we know what is best. We
think we can push the line, wondering what harm could it possibly
do if I do it *my* way just this once! Silly humans!

Chapter 13

Fall led us toward Halloween, which was always a fun time for us. We carved a few pumpkins and painted faces on others. We raked leaves into piles and took turns jumping into the piles with all the neighborhood children. The large pile of leaves looked so soft, but I assure you, it was not for this adult!

A couple of weeks before Halloween that year, I had planned a garage sale. Casey spent the day with my friend, Donna, while I was preparing for the sale. Donna didn't have children, and she loved to spend time with Casey. She would take her for manicures (yes, at age three) and spoil her rotten each time she spent the day with her. At the end of that particular Saturday, she came home with a new set of acrylic paints. Donna had purchased the set along with several pumpkins. Each pumpkin had a different face painted with acrylics, and Casey was very proud of her work! I asked her to put her new paint set away and reminded her that she was only allowed to paint in the kitchen under my supervision. She obediently put the paint set on a shelf in her bedroom and agreed to the terms of arrangement. At the end of the day, she took her bath and laid on the bed with all her stuffed animals, talking to them for about an hour as she told them about her day. I stood out of sight by the door and listened with a huge smile on my face. Ah…the imagination of children!

The next Tuesday was Bible study night. Each Tuesday, Casey would have a babysitter while I went to my small group Bible study. She looked forward to that night because she got to watch one of her movies. That particular night, when I came home, everything seemed to be in order. I took the babysitter home and then got Casey ready for bed. We read stories, said prayers, and I rubbed her back until she fell asleep. Then came the surprise. I walked into my bathroom to get ready for bed, and the shower curtain, the walls, the mirror, the toilet and sink were covered in designs with her acrylic paint. I was so angry! I woke her up and asked her why she would do such a thing. Once again, she just stared at me and gave no answer. Then I spanked her. I put her back to bed and went back to the bathroom to clean it up. But I was so angry, I broke my cardinal rule. I went back in and spanked her again. It took me an hour and a half to clean up the mess. I had to throw away the shower curtain.

After cleaning up the bathroom, as well as myself, I knelt down to say my nightly prayers. I felt so guilty for spanking her that second time. I kept thinking to myself that if anything happened to her during the night, the last thing I did was spank her in anger. And even if nothing did happen to her during the night, I was worried that spanking her in anger would leave a lasting psychological scar on her. (Oh, the guilt parents endure!) So I woke her up, told her I was sorry, asked her for forgiveness, and let her know how much I loved her. She readily forgave me. (Oh, the lessons we can learn from a child!) With a sleepy smile, she added reassurance to her insecure parent, "Mommy, you're so cute. I just love that you're my mommy."

I gave her a big hug and let her know in no uncertain terms that I was so happy to be her mommy. That night, I fell asleep in *her* bed. The next day, she was on the phone with Donna, and I heard her say, "I painted the bathroom for my mommy while she was gone, but she didn't appreciate it. I decorated it real good, but she was *really* mad!" Needless to say, those acrylic paints went into the garbage!

*****

Fall also brought with it a trip to North Carolina for my brother's birthday. We stayed two weeks and went to a family reunion so that Casey could meet all the extended family. She had them eating out of her hand, and they spoiled her rotten. We stayed at Uncle Earl's house for a couple of days, and he pushed Casey in the swing for hours each day we were there. My aunt Mary from Florida also stayed there those two days, and every time she left the house, she came back with a new toy for Casey. Everyone commented on what a wonderful child she was, so loving and kind and always sharing her toys with the other children. She was the hit of the reunion.

I had to humbly agree with them; she was quite special. I felt so fortunate God knit her together with such an easygoing personality. I had studied this fact in college, but until I had my own child, I never truly believed children were born with their own personality, and we, as parents, have only about a 20 to 30 percent "moldability factor." I guess that is why two children raised the same way in the same home can turn out so differently! I was just thankful she was so good-natured. Under my tutelage, without being born with such a personality, she may have turned out to be a nervous wreck!

That year for Halloween, Casey dressed as a ballerina. As a one-year-old, she had been a pumpkin. As a two-year-old, she had been a princess. She continued to have a fetish for dresses and bathing suits or anything like a bathing suit. Being a ballerina allowed her to wear a leotard, and that was much like a bathing suit, so she was happy. Each Halloween, we would go trick-or-treating in the neighborhood and then go to the church for a harvest party. It was always great fun, and we had quite an eventful evening. On the way home, we discussed green peas at length. She had always been enamored with green peas. So on the way home, it was not necessarily unusual for us to be discussing that subject.

"Mommy," she said, "I'm so glad we had green peas for dinner tonight. Green peas make your hair curly, so that's why my hair is so curly…because I love green peas. And it is important that my hair be curly as a ballerina."

"Who told you that?" I inquired.

"Well, Uncle Gary, of course. He knows everything!" (Leave it to my brother to give her information to make our conversations just a bit more interesting!)

When we got home, I gave Casey her bath, and we ended the night watching a television movie called *Snoopy Leaves Town*. Sure enough, Snoopy was getting a new owner and was going to have to leave Charlie Brown and the gang. The gang gave Snoopy a going-away party, and the next day, Snoopy set off for his new home. Charlie Brown was so sad and started crying. About that time, Casey burst out sobbing as well.

"What's wrong?" I asked.

"Mommy, Charlie is so sad. Isn't there anything we can do to help?" She was crying uncontrollably, and I just held her in my lap until, of course, Snoopy came back. Fortunately for Snoopy and Charlie, the condo building where his new home was to be did not allow dogs! Snoopy and Charlie were reunited. What a sweet heart that child had! All she wanted was to make it better for Charlie! She continued to have that gift of empathy for others as she grew up.

*****

Thanksgiving was a time to visit friends, Grandma and Grandpa, and finally Nana and Papa. Since Nana and Papa were our "adopted family" in the city where we lived, they treated us like we were part of their clan, and we never felt like outsiders. We got up early, loaded the car, and off we went for the drive to the first stop. I placed Casey in her car seat and asked her to buckle up. She was trying to ignore me, so I used my very serious tone of voice, "Casey Elizabeth, you buckle that seat belt up."

She glared at me, started to buckle the seat up, and said, "Mommy Elizabeth, you make me so mad!"

I always enjoyed our excursions because the conversations we had were usually quite fun and often memorable. Casey was learning all of her animal sounds, so we practiced them when driving in the car that day.

"How does a cow go?"

Mooo, she would drawl out.

"How does a chicken go?"

Bawk, bawk, bawk.

"How does a doggie go?"

Ruff, ruff.

She was getting quite good at making the sounds for each of the animals. I was constantly trying to think of new animals to introduce to the banter. In the car that morning, I asked her, "How does a giraffe go?"

I wasn't sure myself what sound a giraffe makes, so I was interested to see what she would come up with. She was quiet for so long that finally I looked over at her and asked her again. She responded by hunching her neck down as low as possible and then extending it up as high as she could. We both broke out laughing! To this day, I still don't know what sound a giraffe makes. The neck movement became our joke.

Our first stop that day was at her friend Jenna's house. Her parents had been such a great support to me as a single parent. Casey and Jenna had been friends since they were babies. The two girls were in the bedroom playing when all of a sudden, Jenna ran out looking forlorn.

When her mother asked what was wrong, she said, "Casey wants to play the hurt game."

I called Casey out and asked her if she had indeed said that to Jenna. She sweetly replied, "No, Mommy, I didn't say I wanted to play the hurt game." But I was suspicious, so I thought I'd approach it a bit differently.

"Were you trying to hurt Jenna?" I asked.

This time, with wide eyes, she replied, "Yes, Mommy, it's fun hurting Jenna."

I thought to myself, *Oh no...she takes after my brother!* He picked on me unmercifully growing up. Now genetically the mean streak had passed to my daughter! History! We spent the whole drive to Grandma and Grandpa's discussing how to treat other people, especially your friends!

It had been a long full day by the time we got home from Nana's that night. I ran the water for Casey's bath and told her to take her clothes off and put them in the dirty clothes basket. About that time, the phone rang. I was on the phone with relatives from back east for a bit, and when I got off the phone (which at the time was a landline with a cord in the wall), I yelled down the hallway asking if she was in the bathtub.

She responded, "I've already washed, and I'm out drying off."

As I walked into the bathroom, I was in the middle of telling her that she would have to get back in the tub because we needed to wash her hair tonight, but I stopped with a sudden jolt when she took off the towel, and I noticed that she still had her panties and one sock on. In addition, one leg looked very pale compared to the other. I reached down to examine her leg, which explained why she had on only one sock. On her other leg, she had one of my knee-high stockings on. She had pulled it up to where it bunched in the rolls of fat at her groin. It was bizarre!

I asked her why she had on her panties, one sock, and a stocking. It all seemed quite logical to her as she responded, "Well, my panties were dirty too, and since I was taking a bath, I thought I would go ahead and wash them too. And when I put my clothes in the basket, I saw your stocking. It was dirty too. I couldn't find the other one, so I put on a sock to wash that instead." Already, as a three-year-old, she was trying to kill two (or more) birds with one stone!

Chapter 14

It was a busy season as Christmas approached…always one of our favorite times of the year. Casey was learning to write her alphabet letters, albeit many backwards. It always amazed me. I couldn't write backward that well even if I tried. She practiced writing as we traveled to concerts, pretending she was writing Christmas cards. I had several Christmas concerts that season, and Casey went to all of them with me. We had a large one in California at the Naval Reserve Base. Our team had set up and finished practicing when a marine unit came into the concert hall from a basic training exercise startling us all.

Casey walked up to a group of them, looked at their packs they had laid on the floor, then ran up to the microphone on the stage, and promptly inquired, "Mommy, they have guns and knives! Are these the bad guys?"

After much laughter, of course, all the soldiers had to come up and talk with her at that point. She was once again the bell of the ball!

*****

Each Christmas, we put up a Christmas tree, lights on the house, and a Moravian star. That year, we drove to up into the nearby mountains to cut a live tree from the forest. It was a beautiful day with snow on the ground. We stopped for her first taste of hot chocolate on the way home. We put up the houselights, the star, and decorated the tree to the sound of Christmas carols.

At bedtime, we were both exhausted. We knelt down to pray, and for the first time, Casey said her own prayers; she didn't just repeat after me. She thanked God for the tree, for Aunt Susan and Uncle Gary, and for Mommy. She then thanked God for her daddy and told God it was okay if he decided not to send another daddy. After the amen, I asked her about that.

She looked at me with a long forlorn face and said, "Mommy, we've been asking for a daddy for a long time, and God hasn't sent one yet. Somehow, I don't think he's going to."

I held her in my arms for two whole hours that night after she fell asleep. I had grown up without a father and knew the pain of it. Now it seemed history was repeating itself. I too was very sad.

The next morning, Casey shook me awake in bed and exclaimed, "Mommy, I had the best dream last night! I dreamt ET was holding me, and he wasn't afraid of children! And I wasn't afraid of him. It was so nice, Mommy."

I wondered if it had anything to do with me holding her so long the night before. At breakfast that morning, we had one of our wonderful conversations…this time about television. I asked her what she remembered most about all the television shows she had seen in her short years here on earth. I was expecting something like a certain movie or cartoon or a *Sesame Street* program. Instead, she lowered her voice and very seriously stated, "We'll be right back after these messages!" She even had the right intonations!

I asked her if she knew what "messages" were. She answered, "Sure…it means they're going to check the phone messages." Keep in mind, at that time prior to cell phones, we depended on our answering machines quite a bit!

*****

Christmas shopping created its own problems. I had determined I would never be one of those parents who put their child on a bungee cord, but I was starting to think twice about it. If I let go of her for a moment, she was gone. I panicked in a department store, running down every aisle, yelling her name until I found her. She was standing in the middle of a lingerie rack, feeling the silky material. She calmly looked up at me and stated in a loud voice for all to hear, "*There* you are! You lost me!"

At the grocery store, she would eat the ice from the displays and munch on fruit from the fruit stands when I wasn't looking. At times, she would stuff her pockets with packs of gum while I was unloading the cart. After the gum-stealing happened a second time, we went home and had a *very* serious conversation about stealing! We then took it back to the store, and I made her tell the manager that she had stolen it. The manager handled it fairly well. He thanked her for being honest and smiled. I would have preferred that he threaten to arrest her the next time, but he was too kind.

I thought I had driven home the point about stealing. I *thought* we had an understanding about how serious it was. However, just six days later, I knew I had a deeper problem. Not only did she steal, but she lied about it! I was certain she understood after our previous discussion that stealing was taking something that wasn't hers or something that she had not paid for.

That day, we had been Christmas shopping, and she wanted me to buy her some toys at one of the stores. I told her that she would get a lot of surprises for Christmas, and that we would not be buying anything for her this close to Christmas. She got very angry and screamed, "You don't ever buy me anything! I don't have any toys at home!"

That was so far from the truth; I almost laughed. Instead, I stoically paid for the items at the checkout counter and took her home. As she was getting out of the car in the driveway, a bright bottle of glue dropped out of her pocket. I asked her where she had gotten it, and at least she told me the truth about this particular item as she replied, "At the store."

When I asked if she had stolen it, she replied that she had. I was trying to keep my cool and asked her why she took it. She answered simply, "Because I didn't have any."

Lastly, I asked her if she had taken anything else, and she responded that she hadn't, but there was just something about the sheepish look on her face that made me check her other pocket. Sure enough, there was another bottle of glue. I don't even think she knew exactly what was in the bottle, but it was a bright purple glue, and purple was her favorite color.

I took her inside, spanked her, and explained once again that it was very wrong to steal. I sat her in a corner and told her to think about it for a while. When I went back in her room fifteen minutes later, she was very angry with me and felt she was being punished unjustly. I responded to her that we would have to take it back to the store the next day and tell the lady she had stolen the glue.

And that's what we did. We went back to the store, and I made Casey tell the manager that she had stolen the glue, that she was sorry, and that she would never do it again. The female manager smiled and said, "Oh, that's okay. Isn't she sweet!"

I was spitting mad and replied, "No, she isn't sweet, and no… it is *not* okay."

We marched out of the store with the lady staring open mouthed at us. I was *certain* the lesson had now been learned!

That evening, as I was pulling the covers back to prepare her for bedtime, I discovered a bracelet that she had admired at Kmart earlier in the day when we were picking up some wrapping paper. It was tucked halfway down under the covers. Okay, now I was *really* angry. I called her in the room and held up the bracelet.

"Why did you take this from the store?" I asked.

With a straight face, she replied, "Because I wanted it."

I asked her if she knew it was wrong to take it, and she nodded her head affirmatively. At that point, I was so angry I had to go have my own time-out so that I didn't explode. I told her to sit on the bed until I got back without moving an inch. I went in the other room to cool down and to try to come up with a different plan of action.

When I returned to her room a bit later, she looked very timid. I sat down in front of her and explained, "I am not happy with what you did. Stealing is bad. The Bible says not to steal, and you have done it several times in a row now. If a policeman catches you, he could take you away and punish you. Now, Casey, I'm going to punish you severely for what you've done, and I hope it keeps you from ever stealing again. First, I'm going to spank you because you willfully disobeyed me. Next, you can have no sweets for two whole days. Finally, you have to revert back to riding at all times in the shopping cart while in a store. There will be no walking for you until I feel I can trust you again. Do you understand?"

She replied that she did. At that point, I pulled her pants down and gave her a good whack on her bare bottom. It was the first time I had ever spanked her on her bare bottom, and I'm sure it stung. I felt so badly, and at that point, I knew how God must feel when he has to discipline us for our willful behavior. How often do I want something so badly that I try to obtain it at all costs? I was certain that God was giving me an intimate view of how he feels when I am so willfully disobedient. Yet I could not help but think, *If I love her this much, how much more must he love us!*

I let her cry for a few minutes and then took her in my arms and told her I loved her. I assured her that it was her actions I didn't like, not her. I let her know how much I adored and treasured her, but it was important that she understood actions like that would not be tolerated.

When I asked her if she understood, she merely asked me in return, "Mommy, do you like to spank me when I stealed?" (I wasn't sure this was sinking in at all!) I assured her that I never liked to spank her, but I also promised her that she would get another spanking if she ever stole again. Once again, I assured her that her actions were bad, but she was a wonderful good girl. As we knelt to pray a bit later, I was deflated at how poorly I had obviously delivered the message. She closed her prayer by saying, "God, forgive me for stealing today…and forgive me for being a good girl."

*****

As Christmas drew nearer, the season got busier. Casey would practice writing her name and the names of all our family members. I thought she was Einstein! We baked cookies to take to neighbors and friends, each of us sneaking licks of batter when the other was supposedly not looking. We spent hours in the car driving to concerts or practices and singing Christmas songs. She had a real knack for memorizing words. We also went out at night to look at Christmas lights in the neighborhoods. Her *oos* and *aas* were enough to keep me smiling for weeks, or at least until the next time an alien inhabited her and took away her sweetness…like the time she came home and didn't like the rose on her dress, so she got the scissors and cut it out.

We bought mistletoe and hung it in the doorway to the kitchen. I stood under the mistletoe and told her to come over there so I could give her the traditional kiss that one gives/receives when standing under mistletoe. She danced her way over and puckered her lips. I pecked her on the mouth, and she looked up at me indignantly, "Mommy, that's not the way you kiss. Here's how you do it." She then smashed her lips into mine, twisted her head back and forth, imitating a passionate kiss. She was very proud of herself, and I felt thoroughly kissed. Oh, the things they learn from television!

For Christmas that year, all she said she wanted was a daddy and a Baby Sparkle. Santa didn't quite know how to respond to at least one of those requests. At night, when we said prayers, she continued to ask God to bless her daddy in heaven and to send her a new one very soon. She never really did give up! And I didn't encourage her to give up. After all, I knew that anything was possible with God, and more than anything, I wanted *her* to believe that too. At the same time, I didn't want her to be disappointed if she didn't get a daddy. I told her, "I know that God is preparing just the right person for you and me. It may take a while, but God knows what is best."

As I put her to bed, I thought about what it might mean to have a dad around. My thoughts ran rampant…the thing about your biological dad is you don't get to choose him. You get who you get for good or for bad, but if I got the opportunity to help provide a daddy for Casey, I would make sure that he chose us…not just me but *us*. He wouldn't have to *learn* to love her; he just already would. I would want him to love her as much as I do…well, almost. I didn't think anyone could love her as much as I did, except God. She was the biggest part of me. Life without her at that point would have seemed empty.

Finding a Baby Sparkle proved to be a task almost as difficult as finding a daddy. Baby Sparkle was all the rage that year…a doll that would light up when you hugged her. So I set out on the quest to find the doll, hitting five stores in three hours, maneuvering through heavy traffic. It was two days before Christmas, and I was relieved when I finally located the doll at the fifth store. Casey had been staying with Grandma and Grandpa while I shopped. When I went to pick her up, she was excitedly telling them how Santa was going to bring her a doll whose bow lit up in her hair when you hugged her.

Oh no! The doll I bought had hair that lit up and changed colors when you hugged her. I ran back to the car and looked in the trunk. How could I have made that mistake? I had picked up Miss Sparkles, not Baby Sparkle. Defeat! Tragedy! I had to go on the hunt again. On Christmas Eve, I took Miss Sparkles back to the store and continued to search for the real deal. After hitting another dozen stores, I finally found a brown-skinned Baby Sparkle. I bought it and was flooded with relief.

Christmas morning brought a squeal of delight as she hugged Baby Sparkle. After the first half hour, Baby Sparkle was relegated to the bed and was rarely played with again. No one could take the place of that ugly Baby Amy! Lesson learned: Don't constantly try to get her what she wants. She doesn't know what she really wants. She just thinks she does. Much like us! How many times do we ask God for things that he already knows are not really what we desire?

On New Year's Day that year, we went to a nursing home to visit with the older people there and take some cookies we had made. New Year's Day always brought a bit of sadness to me. It had been a quirky day at our house when I was growing up, and I always thought of my mom on this day. Every New Year's, Momma would fix black-eyed peas and collard greens, and you would eat them whether you wanted to or not! The black-eyed peas were for good health, and the collard greens were for wealth. Somehow, I think she truly believed that if she ate those things every New Year's Day, she would be healthier and a little wealthier.

Casey always brought delight to those at the nursing home. She was just a born ham at that age. Shy was not in her vocabulary. She sang and danced and told silly jokes. That New Year's Day, she dressed in her new Lycra jumpsuit that she got for Christmas. She was so excited to get to wear it finally. She ran around jumping up and down, exclaiming, "See, Mom, I told you I would be able to jump higher in a jumpsuit. I need more of these…look how high I can jump! I'll really be a good gymnast now!"

That enthusiasm carried over to the nursing home residents who were thoroughly captivated that day. On the way home, I asked her if she enjoyed herself. She thought about it for a moment and replied, "Yes, but those people were *real* old!"

I told her that old people were very special, and they were a gift from God, just like babies. I let her know that grandmas and grandpas were a very special gift too.

She looked up at me with serious eyes and said, "Mommy, I hope you never get *that* old."

I smiled and responded, "I hope I *do*!"

Chapter 15

January 14 of that year was the day before the deadline President Bush had given Saddam Hussein of Iraq to withdraw his troops from Kuwait. Americans were braced for war to begin sometime soon, and we all prayed for our leaders and servicemen. Many Christians believed it could be the beginning of the end of times. I could not explain this to Casey at such a young age, and she had difficulty understanding why all the adults were glued to the television or radio. The anxiety of the situation made me restless and nostalgic. My head was filled with selfish thoughts. I so wanted to see Casey grow up and have a loving relationship with Jesus. Even as a young child, she had already asked Jesus into her heart. Perhaps she didn't really understand all of what that meant, but it was done with such purity. I felt God had truly honored that request and would always stay with her. In fact, ever since she was a baby, I had always felt that God had not *one* but *two* angels looking out for her. I distinctly remembered praying when she was born, thanking God for his promise in scripture to provide angels to watch over children. I remembered asking him if he could please provide Casey with two since she had no father and had a handicap of me as a mother. I felt with a certainty in my heart that God's answer had been a resounding yes.

The tension of that day carried into the night, and after I put Casey to bed, I sat there thinking of Momma. I would often think of her, but she had occupied my thoughts throughout this particular day. As I sat in the rocking chair, I remembered the last time I took Casey to see her before she died. She was in the hospital and not expected to live much longer. Momma was so excited to see her. She hugged and kissed Casey with tears in her eyes, and I was praying that Casey would not catch the infectious hepatitis C that Momma had protracted from her last blood transfusion. That picture was indented on my memory…my mom hugging my daughter in the way that I had always wished she had hugged me. She looked at Casey with a love that I had always hoped to see in her eyes when she looked at me. Somehow it was okay, though. I felt in some way I had finally done something good, something that made her proud of me. Casey truly brought a light to Momma's eyes in a way no one else seemed to. I remembered watching Momma and her husband, Bob, say goodbye to each other. Bob was in the hospital at that same time recovering from triple bypass heart surgery. The nurse wheeled him into her room, and I watched as they cried and tried to act normal. Neither could bring themselves to talk of goodbyes or death. But the tears, the emotion, the words of love, the regret, the fear, and the torment in their eyes said it all, and I had to leave the room to keep from bursting into sobs.

I don't think Momma was afraid to die. I think she was ready to go. She had suffered so much, both physically and mentally. I think she just wished we could all go with her. Maybe Jesus felt some of those same sentiments with the disciples in his last days. He was so brave, so sad, so majestic…but ready to accept God's plan. That was the way I saw Momma that day. I hoped I could be as graceful when it was finally my turn.

As I sat there reminiscing that night, I realized that perhaps I loved life too much, for I would hate to leave Casey. I so longed to watch her grow up, to grow with her, and yet I knew that she could not and should not forever fill that empty spot in my life. I knew I would have to let her go sometime, and that deepened the sadness I already felt that day. That time would probably come sooner than I wanted, for there were already days even then when she was not content to sit in my arms for long periods of time. Perhaps God would fill that empty spot in other ways as she grew older. Then it hit me hard. He must be the one to fill that empty spot, and only he could fill it sufficiently.

For now, I clung to God's promise that he would be a father to the fatherless. That included both Casey and me! And he had indeed been a great father! That night, I was just so grateful that I was not alone in the world.

*****

The first Iraqi war came and went quickly as our troops literally stormed Iraq. The pictures of war on television upset Casey, and she had nightmares for about a week. I wondered if she would remember the missiles exploding or the bloody picture of a man torn apart by such an explosion. I saw it disturbed her.

That war-torn world on television must have looked very strange from a three-year-old's perspective! We talked about how we needed to pray for our soldiers, and her question revealed a depth of perception that could only be seen through the eyes of an innocent child. "Mommy, which soldiers should we pray for? Just ours? They all seem to be getting hurt one way or another?" That was a tough question to answer!

Our band wrote and recorded a song that was used as background music for the *Desert Storm* television special on the war. How very odd hearing your music on the television and radio! By that time, we had had a few songs that had made it to the airways. My alarm was set on a Christian radio station, and more than once, I woke up to me singing. It was surreal!

A couple of weeks later, the war was seemingly forgotten, and everyone was back to their usual routines, feeling safe again, discussing the trivialities of life. Casey and I played kickball until she was exhausted from "running the bases." At that time, she would bend over, place her hands on her thighs and tell me, "Mom, this is how you're supposed to rest. All the football players do this and basketball players too." (It opened my eyes to how much sports we watch on television!)

We retreated into the house, and she promptly picked up the phone and pretended to talk to her daddy. When she finally returned the phone to its cradle, it suddenly rang. Without missing a beat, she answered, "Hello…no, she's busy right now. May I help you? No, you can't talk to him. My dad died when I was just a baby, and I don't have one right now." Then she hung up.

My heart would just break for her sometimes. My love for her was so great. I wanted the very best for her…the best of everything, including a family. I briefly reflected on how much more God must want the best for us. Even at times when he doesn't seem to be taking the action we think he should, he is always there and always wants to provide the best for us. As I always told Casey, "He has great plans for you, plans to give you a future and a hope, not just to give you good things but to give you your heart's desire."

*****

Our daily conversations continued to entertain and, at times, intrigue me. Her mind was developing, just as her body was growing and extending. There was a time when I actually wondered if her arms would ever grow long enough to reach the top of her head so that she could brush her own hair or if her legs would ever grow into the rolls of fat at the top or if her neck would ever grow longer or if it would it always just sit on her chest.

As she started to lengthen out physically, her mind continued to grow and expand as well. Often when we drove in the car, I tried to teach her to sing a "round" with me. We would start by singing together "row, row, row, your boat" together a few times. Then I would start it and point to her when she should start. By the end of the first line, she was *always* singing with me! We used to laugh and laugh. I sang to her almost every night after we read stories and said prayers. Usually, the last song I sang would be "Hush, Little Baby, Don't You Cry." I would continue to make up rhyming words and phrases until she fell asleep.

Sometimes our talks were about lessons she could learn. At other times, it seemed to be about lessons I could learn!

"Mommy, my friend, Michaela, pulls my hair sometimes, but that's just because she's a little girl. And sometimes she pulls it twice, and *then* I pull hers back."

I responded, "Well, that's not a very nice way to respond. I'm not sure that Jesus would want you to pull her hair in return like that."

She quickly replied, "Oh no, Mommy, her daddy told me to do it that way. He said to ask her to stop when she did it once. And if she did it twice, he told me to pull her hair...real hard. I don't think Jesus would mind since her daddy told me to."

She continued to grow even more intuitive as a young child. I was rarely able to hide my feelings from her if something was bothering me. One day, I was having a particularly sad day. As I drove along the road on my way to do an errand, I was praying that God would lighten the load on my heart.

She looked over at me in the car and asked, "Mommy, what are you doing?"

"I'm praying," I said.

"Well, that's a funny thing to do in a car. Why are you doing that?"

"Well, little missy," I replied, "You can pray to God anytime, anyplace, and he hears you and sees you."

"Yeah, I know that, Mommy! It's because he lives right *here*," she said as she pounded the place on her chest under which her heart lies. "But, Mommy, why does Jesus have a toy on his head in all the pictures?"

I had to think about that one for a minute...a toy? Then I got it! "No, that's not a toy, Casey. That's a halo. It's a symbol of his holiness and him living in heaven."

"No, Mommy!" she exclaimed. "He doesn't live in heaven. He lives right here in my heart!"

How can you argue with that? People need to *stop* drawing halos over Jesus's head! Our conversation cheered me right up, and I continued to pray as we drove along the road that God would fill her with his love, and that it would be an attribute she would possess throughout her whole life. I prayed that she would always know that Jesus lives in her heart.

But I also prayed very selfishly that we would always remain the closest of friends. I knew that someday she would probably leave and marry her husband, and then he would become her best friend. Yet my hope was that our love for each other would never cease to grow. Every single day, it was a routine. One of us would say, "I love you." And the other would reply, "I love you *more*." She was such a fulfillment for me, yet I realized even then that she could not be my life. I would have to give her room to grow, to be her own person… room to be all she can be, even if it separates us. I knew I should not and could not continue forever to build my life around her, but I cherished those days when she was little, and I grew scared at times of how quickly the days seemed to pass. She would grow up, and I would grow old. One of my greatest fears was that I would grow old alone. But I hoped, as I grew older, to be like the Velveteen Rabbit. I just wanted to be hugged and loved every day by her until all my fur wore off…even if I was ugly to everyone else.

*****

Casey continued to pray for a daddy, and she talked about it often. It seemed as she drew closer to her four-year-old birthday, the more fervently she prayed. Her prayers became very specific. "Dear God, please bring a daddy real soon. Let him love me and love Mommy and love You. And let him be handsome and smart. And let him like to do sports for Mommy and me. And I would like it if he thought Mommy and I were very, very special. And he can have whatever kind of hair you want and whatever color of eyes you want. He can even be short, but I don't think Mommy would like him to be shorter than her."

After prayers, I asked why she was being so detailed in her prayers these days. She responded, "Well, Mommy, my Sunday school teacher said to be 'pacific'…that means to tell God exactly what your heart desires, so that's what I'm doing." From the mouths of babes!

But as the final days prior to her fourth birthday approached, she was beginning to get discouraged again. It was Valentine's Day, and the day started out well. She ran into my bedroom, giving me kisses, and told me to go brush my teeth to get rid of the elephant breath. There was to be a big party at preschool today, and Casey looked so beautiful. Her long hair was curly, and she dressed in a red plaid skirt with a white shirt trimmed in red, sporting her red patent leather shoes and tights with red hearts.

I cooked a delicious Valentine's dinner that evening for my favorite valentine, Casey. We feasted on her favorite macaroni and cheese with baked ham slices. All in all, it was a good day until bedtime. She said her usual prayers, asking for a daddy, and then got in bed and burst out crying. I had no idea what was wrong and was desperately trying to console her.

"Tell Mommy what's wrong," I prompted. My heart was breaking as the tears streamed down her face.

She looked at me with such a desperate face. "Mommy, when will Jesus and God come to our house for real?"

I emphatically told her they already did live here for real…right in our hearts. But she replied, "No, Mommy, I mean for real, not make believe. I need somebody with skin!"

Her discouragement was difficult to address. It was hard enough to address this type of discouragement with an adult. Where is God when you need him? Why does he feel so distant? Why doesn't he answer my prayers? Is he really there? Really listening? How could I assure her that God is real, not make believe? How could I convince her that he truly is here with us even when we can't see or can't seem to feel him? I tried to explain the best I could, but she was not to be consoled at that moment.

"No, he's not real…if he was real, he would have brought us a daddy by now. It's like making a wish, Mommy. It's not really real!"

It broke my heart. I felt helpless! I didn't want her to believe that loving and believing in God was dependent upon getting our wish list or having prayers answered the way we wanted. I didn't know what else to do except hold her and assure her that God is real, he hears our prayers, and he loves us more than we could ever imagine. She cried herself to sleep, and I remained kneeling on the floor by her bed in prayer. The tears ran down my own face as I poured my heart out.

"Oh, God, please hear our prayers and be merciful to us. I'm running out of answers. I need help. She's never known a father, and yet there is something inside her that is missing a father terribly. Please be her father until you can give her one. I know that if you are the only father she ever has, it can be enough. Please be very real to her! I see the ache in her when her friends run into the arms of their fathers. I see a longing that even I, a mother who loves her so deeply, cannot fill. She knows I love her more than anything imaginable, but I cannot be a father. I cannot be a man whose strong arms lightly pick her up and whose beard scratches at her delicate cheek. I cannot smell like a man or play like a man or flirt with her like a man. I can only be Mommy and hope that will be enough until you bring a man into her life. I know in your Word you promise to be a father to the fatherless, and I feel comfort in that. But, oh God, she doesn't feel that comfort right now. She needs skin. She needs to feel his arms, to smell his hair, to hear his laughter, to rest in his lap, to nudge her head in his shoulder. She needs to feel the security that males can bring to a household. God, I thought holidays were just tough on me. But now I know they are just as tough on her. She says very little, but she is always blue on holidays. Please let her feel your arms around her. Let her hear you whisper in her ear that everything is all right. Let her feel the security that only you can give. And, God, please do it soon."

Chapter 16

Casey's fourth birthday party was nearby, and when it came, it seemed to last for two weeks. But by the time it arrived, I was happy to have the lengthy distraction. I had come home late from a concert in California a week and a half before Casey's birthday. Casey had stayed with Nana and Papa this trip, and I had returned home to an empty house and a day-old paper on the front porch. To unwind from the trip, I decided to read some of the paper before going to bed. On the front page of the sports section was a huge article about women's athletics at the university in town and how I was the cause for all its woes and losing teams. It had been more than six months since I had stepped down from my position there as the main administrator of women's collegiate sport programs. I couldn't believe what I was reading. I guess I shouldn't have been surprised to be blamed since I was no longer there to defend myself, but still, it hurt deeply. I wanted to hide in a hole and never come out. No, actually I wanted to sue, but I knew that was the wrong action to take. I cried most of the night and went to pick Casey up the next day with red swollen eyes.

Nana and Papa had already seen the article and had discussed it a bit with Casey. When I walked in to get her, she ran to me, threw her arms around me, and said, "It's okay, Mommy, I'll take care of you."

We went home, built a fire, and Casey sat in my lap on the couch most of the day, hugging me at frequent intervals. I cried most of the day and felt too embarrassed to go out of the house. Scripture says we are to let God vindicate and protect us, but it was so hard to sit there and take no action. Reporters from the media called and left messages. I never returned them. Finally, I unplugged the phone. I kept thinking of when Jesus said if someone slaps you on the cheek, turn and let him hit the other side too. I felt as though I had been punched in the face, and I wasn't real sure I wanted to take the chance that someone might punch me again. Nevertheless, I decided to trust God to protect me.

For the next few days, Casey continued to console me. I'm not sure she fully understood what was happening, but she understood her mom was upset. She would gently touch my cheek with her hand and tell me she loved me, and that everything would be all right. It seemed odd that an almost four-year-old could bring such comfort and peace.

There were not words to describe how much I loved her or how much she meant to me. She was growing more beautiful each day, inside and out. During these gloomy days, she did her best to cheer me. She made her bed (sort of), picked up her toys, used the Windex on the glass table tops and even attempted to vacuum. Just the week before, I had discussed her being old enough to start having weekly chores. So all but the vacuuming was part of her regular weekly chores. If she did her chores, she got an allowance of ten pennies. I wanted to teach her early about tithing. So each time she got her allowance, she learned to put nine of the pennies in one bank and one penny in "God's bank."

That particular week, after I gave her the allowance, she said, "Don't forget, Mommy, we have to put one of these in the God bank. And do you think that maybe one day, Jesus would like a bank too?" Once again, the topic of the Trinity arose. I tried to explain that Jesus was God's son, and he was a part of God.

"Like I'm a part of you?" she asked.

"Sort of…but even more so. It's like God took part of himself and sent Jesus to earth because he loved us so much."

But the concept still seemed to be too much for her to process. I tried to explain that it was like ice and water being the same thing, but that still didn't get the point across clearly. Explaining the Trinity would have to wait for yet another day!

The days continued to be depressing. I still didn't want to go out of the house. Club Med was advertising a "kids go free" campaign, so I decided we could use a trip out of town for a while during this stressful time of media pounding. On a whim, I decided we would go to Club Med Ixtapa for a week. Casey's flight was free, and there was no extra charge for her at the club. It was a last-minute deal that seemed perfect for us, and a great way to celebrate near her birthday. It was also an escape from the recent press situation.

For me, the week was filled with windsurfing, sailing, swimming, snorkeling, tennis, and competing in fun events set up for adults. Casey went to kid's club each day and spent her days playing in the ocean or the pool, catching crabs, going on boat rides, and making crafts. In late afternoons and evenings, the two of us played in the ocean, went to trapeze shows, played games, blindly swung at piñatas, and went to dinner shows.

I had learned to sail that week at the club, and I took Casey out on a small sailboat late one afternoon. The wind came up, and the waves got higher. Casey looked at me with more terror each passing minute. I tried to stay calm, but I too felt very uncomfortable. Tacking back was a challenge. By the time we returned, I don't think I could have talked her into another sailboat ride for years, even if I had wanted to.

All in all, it was a wonderful trip, except for two things. First, Casey got a stomach bug from drinking the water and had uncontrollable diarrhea for the last couple of days. She would stop and stand in one place, and the diarrhea trail would run down her legs to the beach, the floor, or wherever we happened to be at the time. She was so embarrassed and would start crying each time.

Secondly, on the way home, as we were going through customs, we were detained. The agents seemed to think I was a prime suspect for being a drug smuggler…young woman, seemingly unemployed, yet able to travel to a foreign country. The agents took our luggage and literally ripped it apart, even cutting through the lining of the suitcases. I was just hoping they were not going to check bodily orifices on the two of us. Not only would it have been uncomfortable, but they might have been surprised with something unplanned coming from Casey! She still suffered with stomach issues. We missed our connecting flight to Los Angeles and had to stay in a hotel for the night but finally made it home the next day.

When we returned, there were numerous birthday parties for Casey over the next week—Grandma and Grandpa, Nana and Papa, our friend, Donna, and our friends, Mike and Anita. As we went from party to party, she would ask if she was going to be five yet at the next party. *Whew!* She was spoiled to the core, receiving more toys than we could pile in her closet and toy box—skates, dolls, books, movies, makeup, and nail polish for kids, and several bathing suits. (She still had a fetish for bathing suits!) You could always pick out the gifts that came from people who had no children! No sane adult who has had children would give a preschooler makeup, nail polish, permanent markers, little girl high heels, or noisemakers! At least, not if they liked the parent!

I was "partied out" and exhausted after the trip, but at least the media frenzy had died down. That next Sunday, a male friend from church, Jason, called to ask if he could take Casey and I to dinner for her birthday. I politely declined, but Casey overheard me and insisted on speaking with him.

She took the receiver from me and promptly informed Jason, "I would love to go to dinner with you, even if my Mommy doesn't want to." (Talk about embarrassing!) The two of them made the arrangements, and Jason was on his way to pick Casey up in half an hour. As soon as she hung up the phone, she raced off to the bathroom, exclaiming, "I have to go brush my teeth so I don't have elephant breath!" The two of them went to McDonald's for dinner, and Casey came home with more presents! The kid had a bit of weasel in her!

Casey developed a new fetish as a four-year-old...shoes. It didn't exactly supersede her bathing suit fetish, but it came close. Often times when we would visit friends, Casey would sneak off to the parent's bedroom and start trying on the mom's shoes. She was possessed by high heels! We had many a discussion about invading other people's closets!

Each day, rain or shine, hot or cold, she would put on a bathing suit, even if it was under her regular clothes. She informed me that she was quite capable of dressing herself, and there were many days in the next few weeks where she attempted to do just that. She would put on a bathing suit, a pair of her new birthday high heels, comb her hair, put on some makeup, paint her fingernails, and paint lipstick over half her lower face. She would then walk into my room to state she was ready for the day! "Don't I look beautiful, Mommy?" I'm not sure where she got this "girlie" nature from—certainly not from me! As a parent, I learned to pick and choose my battles. So I would merely have her put on some clothes over the bathing suit and clean up the lipstick from her face before leaving the house. It was an adventure!

Casey soon learned to skate using her birthday Fisher-Price skates. They allowed one to adjust how much the skates would actually roll. She caught on quickly, falling only twice the first day. Learning to jump rope proved to be a much greater challenge. She was determined to learn both skills before Uncle Gary and Aunt Susan came to visit. And she did. He was very proud of her, and it was so wonderful to see how much she loved him.

The highlight of the visit (for me) was when Casey walked in on Uncle Gary while he was urinating in the bathroom. It was usually just us two girls in the house, and Casey was used to walking into any room she pleased at any time. She still had no sense of boundaries. She thought it was just fine to walk in the bathroom to talk to Uncle Gary if she wanted, and she did. I don't think I had ever seen my brother blush with embarrassment before. It was a long awaited treat!

After he and Aunt Susan left to return to North Carolina, Casey was sad. We built a fire, and she sat in my lap in the rocking chair with her head on my chest. After a while, she looked up at me and said, "Mommy, maybe Uncle Gary could be our daddy!" (Oh boy!)

I tried to explain that he was my brother and couldn't be her daddy, but she didn't seem to grasp that concept. She was just disappointed. There had finally been a male around with skin for a while!

As we both contemplated and watched the fire, I could tell her mind was chewing on something else. When I asked about it, she inquired, "Mommy, what will you name me when I grow up?" I told her that her name would always be Casey Elizabeth. I was curious as to why she thought her name would change. She replied that Aunt Susan had told her that she used to be Susan Carter, but now she was Susan Carter Hope. I explained that when you get married, you can choose to take the last name of your husband if you'd like.

"Well, what did your name used to be, Mommy?"

"It's always been the same. I didn't change it," I replied.

"Well, why not? Didn't you like daddy's last name?"

"Of course, I liked it! It's your last name, and I really liked it! I just had to sign my name a lot at work, and I didn't want to sign a long name like that so many times a day. It was a lot easier to write my simple short name," I explained.

"Oh, okay...well, maybe I'll be Gary when I grow up," she replied. "I really like that name! And it's short!"

*****

Casey continued to experience new adventures as a four-year-old. She rode her first Jet Ski, went camping, and learned more about boys. She held her first real human baby and was enthralled with it. She kept commenting that the baby was just as big as her Baby Amy. (Yes, the dreadfully ugly Baby Amy was still around!) She also learned to take a shower. She was a bit intimidated by the shower at first and wanted no part of it. She was afraid the water would get in her eyes, so we put her swim goggles on her as we both jumped in together the first time.

As a four-year-old, she went to her first circus, rode an elephant, went to the balloon races, drove a real car (yes!), and had her first dentist appointment. She had her teeth cleaned and polished, as well as a fluoride treatment and impressions made. Other than gagging on the retainer they inserted with the fluoride treatment, she did well. But for at least two weeks after, she would constantly lick her teeth and ask, "Mommy, do you think I've eaten off all the polish yet?" I kept assuring her the polish would last several more months.

That summer also required getting updated on her shots, which was *not* fun. The polio vaccine went well. But giving her the actual shots was like trying to hold a snake down to extract venom. It did not go well for anyone, especially the doctor. He dropped the needle once and was getting frustrated with all the screaming and squirming. When it was all over, she displayed her growing linguistic skills, letting both the doctor and me know exactly how she felt.

"You're a great big 'hippopopotamus,' and I don't like you, Mr. Doctor. You are *not* a cool dude. And, Mommy, you just sat there in the waiting room before we came in, reading your 'mazagine,' telling me nothing would hurt bad. I'm not happy with you, and you are *not* a cool dudette. I don't even want to go for the 'hangaber' you promised. I want to go home!"

*****

Casey continued to travel with me and the singing group for most of our concerts. We did a lengthy trip through the Seattle area, and Casey had great fun. She took her first fishing trip, caught her first fish, and we cooked it up and ate it for dinner. We visited the Space Needle, rode the hobby horses, and visited numerous parks and playgrounds.

During the long car ride home over several days, we worked on learning opposites and rhyming words. After a day or so, she caught on, and it became a fun game.

As we finally pulled into our driveway, she looked up at me and asked, "Mommy, can we see Ron?" It was the first time she had asked about him in a long while. It broke my heart. I knew she missed his company. I tried to explain to her that Ron had lied to Mommy and had broken her heart into tiny pieces, so we wouldn't be seeing him again.

The tears started rolling down her cheeks as she replied, "But, Mommy, he didn't hurt me. Why can't he just come over to visit me?"

I didn't have the heart to disappoint her anymore that day, so I told her I would think about it. I hoped that one day, she would understand and not hold it against me for cutting Ron from our lives. At that time, I wasn't sure if either of us would ever get over it. Each time I saw him and each time his name came up, it brought a fresh wave of pain.

It had been a long couple of weeks, and we were both glad to get home to our own beds. But sleep was not easy for me that night. Perhaps her sleep had not been so peaceful either. The next morning, she awoke and came into my room with big sad blue eyes and said, "Mommy, I want to go home with my daddy."

"Do you know where your daddy is?" I asked.

"Yes, he's in heaven with Jesus, but I want to visit him."

"Well, honey," I explained, "when we die, we will get to go to heaven and see him...and Grandma Colvin too. He and Grandma Colvin probably talk with each other often, but right now, we can't visit."

But she was not to be consoled. The tears flowed again. We got down on our knees and once again prayed for a daddy. As we stood up, she was so discouraged and disheartened. I felt like a total failure that I couldn't relieve her loneliness for a father. Once again, I had to trust God that he would work it out, and that she wouldn't be "scarred for life." After my childhood, I so wanted a normal, bland, everyday family life for her, but that was not to be. I could only rest in the fact that I knew God had a very special place in his heart for widows and orphans. Yet at times, neither of us felt very special. Some "skin" would have been nice!

Chapter 17

As spring rolled into May, Casey and I prepared for a short-term mission trip to Turkey. Both of us were very excited to visit that part of the world. Casey was allowed to come with me because it was a missionary conference that included all family members. As part of my service, I would be preparing a musical presentation with the children of the missionaries. At the end of the conference, there was to be a concert for the missionaries and their families.

The trip over was gratefully uneventful. By now, Casey was a seasoned traveler. We arrived in Ankara, Turkey, the day after we left the States...two very tired girls. After visiting with a local missionary for a day, we took off for Izmir, Turkey by car. It was several hours away, and we were still jet-lagged from the long trip over. But the lure of the beautiful Mediterranean Sea when we arrived was too much to ignore. We checked into the hotel, unpacked, and headed down to the seaside. It was a glorious ethereal blue. We drew quite a few stares on the beach. There we were two light-haired, light-skinned women in a very Muslim country. At that time, women in Turkey wore burkas and were covered head to toe, even in a seaside town. Although it was a tourist city by the seaside, few Westerners vacationed there. So we stood out like sore thumbs. Our dresses were fairly long, but our heads and arms were uncovered in the almost ninety-five-degree heat.

From the very first day, Casey was not enamored with Turkish culture. She didn't like the food. She didn't like the way men stared at us. She didn't like the way women and children would not look her in the eye or say hello to her. She didn't like that she had to wear dresses each day. And she really didn't like that she couldn't frolic around all day in her bathing suit. But she fit right in with the missionary children, and by the end of the ten days, she had made fast friends and was sad to leave them. She was wise enough even at four years old to know that she would probably never see them again.

But her spirits lifted as soon as we boarded the boat for a Greek island. The Greek islands had always been my favorite place to visit ever since I did a European walkabout at the age of twenty-six for several months. I couldn't wait to share the experience with Casey. After arriving on the island, we checked into the hotel, rented a scooter, and took off to explore the island. The thrill of riding on that scooter next to cliffs overlooking the Mediterranean and viewing all the majestic white-washed buildings left a lasting impression on her. She loved the food, loved the people (who doted on her), loved that she could ride on a scooter with her mom all over the island, and loved that she could wear a bathing suit all day long if she wanted to.

After a few days in that wonderland, we boarded a boat to take us back to Istanbul. We spent two days sightseeing there before heading home, but the sights did not make up for the oppressiveness we felt as we walked the streets. Most Westerners were in groups or at least accompanied by men. Casey and I were on our own, and we both felt out of place as we walked the streets, even in the tourist areas. After the freedom of Greece, we felt conspicuous and even a bit unsafe. It made leaving to go home easier. We were both anxious to depart a place where women seemed so obviously undervalued.

After boarding the plane, Casey sat quietly for a long while. I let her be for a while as she was always a processor; she had to think something through before she was ready to talk about it. She had been that way since she was two. Eventually, I asked her what she was thinking about. With the pluckiness of a child, she responded, "Mommy, I wish we could have had our dog here with us."

"Why do you say that, honey? We don't have a dog!"

"I know, Mommy, but we need a dog. Nana says they are therapy."

Just for fun. I asked her what therapy meant, and she replied, "That's when people need to learn things from dogs that they don't learn from people."

I wasn't quite sure how to respond to that, so I asked, "Well, why do you think a dog would have been helpful to have here in Turkey?"

"Because my dog would have been here to like me and love on me and accept me just like I am. Maybe he could have taught these people a thing or two! He could have showed them how to love too…because, Mommy, you know dogs don't need words to show they care. So it wouldn't have mattered that he couldn't speak Turkey."

That logic made perfect sense to me!

*****

The remainder of that summer was filled with swimming, canoe trips, playgrounds, concert trips, and friends. Almost every Friday, "Aunt" Ter Ter and "Uncle" Fritz came by the house to give her a foot massage, a leg rub, and a manicure. Uncle Fritz would read her stories before bedtime. This became a ritual that summer. And as serendipity would have it, Casey also got her first dog that summer. Nana showed up at the doorstep one day in June with London, the new golden Labrador. I was not exactly thrilled to have a dog. I already had a fetish with vacuuming. I drove everyone crazy because I didn't want them to walk on my carpet after I vacuumed. And I vacuumed about three times a day, making sure the carpet lines were perfect.

Nana thought it best to treat my compulsive behavior with a dog. Casey was thrilled! I was a bit angry. London had been trained to be a seeing eye dog but had failed the final test. He just couldn't discern when to cross a street and would constantly walk out in the street, ignoring traffic. I was not actually sure how bright London was, but we came to love him anyway. He was a bit hyperactive and dug up my yard, but he was potty trained.

London became Casey's constant companion, sleeping with her each night. He would not budge from her side until she got up each morning. He was her protector, and she was his playmate and best friend. Each day, she woke to give him lots of love, and she played constantly with him. His biggest talent was his ability to hold three tennis balls in his mouth at once. He looked like the cartoon of a widemouthed frog! She quickly forgave him when he chewed up her new kiddie pool and beach ball. But when he took a bite of Baby Amy…well, that was where she drew the line. She spanked him hard and refused to talk to him the rest of the day. Baby Amy was patched up with some superglue and covered with a Band-Aid.

We also planted a garden that summer in the backyard, and Casey had her own little patch that year where she planted her choices. We could hardly wait to see them grow. She had finally given up the habit of eating dirt clods, so it was now safe to allow her in the garden to help. It was exciting each week to see the sprouts grow larger. It made us feel like a part of nature, and everything seemed to be growing well, except the asparagus (which I later discovered I had planted upside down). Finally, eating out of our garden brought the greatest satisfaction to both of us—corn, carrots, green beans, onions, lettuce, tomatoes, and even a cantaloupe or two.

Gardening brought back so many memories of when I was a child living with my grandparents. My grandfather grew just about everything we ate. My grandmother canned the extras for the winter months. He grew all sorts of fruits and vegetables, and the planting season was a family affair. Each year, my grandfather hired an old black man with a mule and a hand plow to make the furrows, and we participated in an assembly line. My grandfather poked a hole in the furrow with a stick every few inches, and my grandmother placed a seed or a plantlet. My brother followed with a bucket of water and filled the hole with water. I came last and covered the hole with fresh dirt. We watched the corn grow higher than our heads over the summer months, and the pea patches grew so dense snakes would hide in them. There were even grapevines for eating and making jelly. Thinking of all the strawberries, melons, peaches, figs, and apricots can still make my mouth water even today. In the fall, there were potatoes and nuts. Some of my most vivid memories were coming home from school with the permeating smell of sweet potatoes and peanuts roasting in the fireplace.

My grandparent's house where we lived was very, very old with worn hardwood floors and a few threadbare carpets. The ceilings were twenty-five feet high, and spiders would congregate on the ceiling in corners. I was terrified they would drop down on me in the night while I was sleeping. We had no central heat and no air-conditioning. Summers were sweltering hot and humid. And in the winter, you could see your breath in the mornings; it was so cold. We had a couple of kerosene heaters, and when we took a bath, we carried a portable one into the bathroom to keep from freezing. The house had virtually no insulation, and when the wind blew, the house would sing. Or at times, it seemed as if it was howling when the wind was particularly fierce. We slept under homemade quilts during the winter, piled so thick that I could barely move under the covers. In the summer, all the windows were open to bring in what little breeze there might have been.

The house had a wraparound front porch with a porch swing that hung from the rafters. I would sit in that swing for hours and watch people walk by, traffic pass, and rainstorms flash. It was my favorite place to sit. There was a chinaberry tree in the front yard (which was all dirt) that stood near the road. Often, I climbed the tree and hid amongst the leaves and branches and picked chinaberries to throw at passing cars.

The old barn on the property was my exploration cave. It was filled with all sorts of old odds and ends and was always a bit scary to enter. You never knew what creatures might be lurking in there. Boxes and items were piled so high; it seemed that a child could never get through exploring everything. Dust and spiderwebs loomed in the darkness, and there was no electricity. It required courage to enter. It was the perfect "haunted house" for a child. The outside of the barn had a basketball hoop on it where, together with my brother, his friends, and my nanny's children, we would shoot hoops when weather allowed. Sometimes even my mom would shoot a few hoops with us!

I referred to Hazel as my nanny, but in reality, she was a house-keeper and cook who worked for my elderly grandparents in exchange for food and low wages, but she was also like part of the family. I loved Hazel! She was there when I woke up each morning and there when I got home from school each day. She was a tall well-built, single black woman with seven children and a marvelous loving heart. She woke me each morning with a hug that reeked of the Salem cigarettes she smoked, but I didn't mind. Skin was skin, and I loved the hugs!

I was not allowed to go to school in the morning until I had my cup of coffee and bacon. I'm quite certain that I would have been at least six feet tall had my growth not been stunted by drinking coffee from such a young age! During the summer, it seemed that we had fried corn bread, potatoes, and fried pork fat back almost every single day for lunch. It's a wonder I didn't die of a heart attack by the time I was eighteen. Much of my protein consumption was pork fat because it was cheap. And pork fat was added to everything to make it tast-ier—green beans, field peas, turnips, corn, soups, collards, potatoes, you name it.

As children, most of the year, we played outdoors from morning until after dark, except during school hours. Besides shooting basket-ball hoops, we rode bikes without helmets, skated in the streets with cars, played tag with the lightning bugs prancing around us, climbed trees, played pickup sticks and jacks, and literally ran all over town with no adult supervision. Aah, those were the days. On especially boring days in the summer, I caught beetle bugs, tied a string around one of their tiny legs, and watched them fly in a circle around me like a toy airplane. Eventually, the string would slip off, or the leg would break. We caught butterflies and lightning bugs and kept them in jars as pets until they died. And somehow it never occurred to us that it might be animal cruelty.

As I grew older, I played catch with my brother, passed foot-balls, and continued to ride bicycles, skate, and play basketball. In the summer, I gave up bugs and graduated to stealing watermelons from surrounding farms and busting them on a country road, eating the hearts out.

My brother and cousins shot BB guns until my cousin shot my tooth out. I was rushed to the local dentist who extracted the remainder of the front lower tooth. I was embarrassingly snaggletoothed as a twelve-year-old for about six months until the hole filled in. In the end, it was a blessing. My bottom teeth were so crowded that all the teeth were crossed up. Once that tooth was extracted, the remaining teeth straightened out very nicely. But every dentist I ever visited asked me what happened to that fourth tooth that was supposed to be in between my eyeteeth! This was one of my first lessons that something good can come from a tragedy. Sometimes you have to go through humiliation, embarrassment, and awkwardness. But eventually, you come out better in the end!

Chapter 18

The thought processes of my child never ceased to amaze me. To watch her mind absorb and grow and process was more entertainment than a movie. Her innocence at times and lack thereof at other times continued to keep me amused that year. I almost envied the simplicity of her four-year-old thought patterns and wondered more than once how, as adults, we get so convoluted and complicated. And then I remembered…oh yeah, we learned to be that way! I began to realize that my child's spongelike mind picked up far more than I probably realized. To a child, experiences are merely that at first, they are neither good nor bad; they just are…until someone tells them it is good or bad! Then they have to make a choice. Do I want to do that again knowing it's bad? Or do I want to choose to stay away from that behavior? I certainly did not teach her how to be bad! That came naturally. Oh yes, I learned so much that year!

At that time, we had an alcoholic neighbor, Randy, who cursed at everything and everyone when he was drinking. We tried to stay out of his way, but he was retired and was always outside. He was in "Casey's space." I think he actually enjoyed watching her play. Casey was just about the only person Randy was nice to on a regular basis. As I called to Casey one summer evening to come in for dinner, she promptly headed for the door. She had been outside playing with her ever-present pal, London. Dogs were rarely on leashes then. She called for the dog to come in as well, but London was busy sniffing around. All of a sudden, I heard her yell, "London, get the hell in the house!"

Taken aback, I asked her where she learned to use language like that.

"Oh, Mom, it's okay. Randy says that all the time."

So we had to have a long talk about good and bad language and cursing. It was difficult to explain to a four-year-old why an adult was allowed to say and do things without being scolded. But I tried to make it clear that it was not necessarily allowable for others to do and say the same things without consequences. And I also made a mental note. We are all being watched by someone who is taking cues from how we act!

There were more poignant times when her dialogue really made me think. One day, as we were riding in the car going to swim lessons, she was eating potato chips. But she was eating them in a strange fashion. She would put one in her mouth and chew it very slowly before swallowing. The next one, she would chew very rapidly and force it down quickly. I noticed a pattern developing and asked her what she was doing.

"Well, Mommy, I needed a snack before I went to swim, and you gave me some chips. Well, I thought Jesus might want a snack too. He's inside me you know? So, first, I eat a chip, and then Jesus eats the chip after me. I have to chew his chip a little, but I'm trying to get it down there as whole as I can so that he can have something to chew." (The mind of a child…oh, if we could only visualize Jesus in us like that each day and try to please him!)

I learned that at the tender age of four, she was starting to contemplate exactly what she was saying when she prayed. I had taught her some prayers to say as a child. She repeated them with me until she learned them. One evening before dinner, she said one of those prayers before our meal. "God is good. God is great. Let us thank him for our food and bless it to our bodies…pssst, Mommy, what's a body?" From then on, we gave up rote prayers and started truly talking to God.

From the time Casey was two years old, it had been a ritual at dinner that I would ask her to tell me one new thing she had learned that day. She was usually quick to answer with at least one thing, sometimes more. If not, I would teach her something new right then. But there were also times when she would teach me something.

"Mommy, I'm going to tell you something that *you* can learn today. When you burp and you don't want to burp out loud, you can try to swallow it, but it will come back up. You can try to force it down, but it will *always* come back up. You may not see it or hear it, but you sure can smell it! So you may as well just burp out loud!"

*****

Samuel was one of Casey's best friends growing up. He was the adopted son of our neighbor across the street and had been born in Korea. He was the same age as Casey and had a major crush on her. Casey was infatuated with Samuel's eyes and just wanted to know why his eyes were so pretty and different. She rather liked him as well, but I think it was mostly because she could boss him around. He constantly asked if she could come live at his house. Since I said a firm no to that, his parents and I agreed they could have supervised sleepovers. When they were at Samuel's, Casey slept in one of the bunk beds. And when Samuel stayed at our house, he would sleep on the floor next to Casey's bed in a tent and sleeping bag.

I checked in on them every few minutes while they were awake. I was still worried about Casey being on the end of her "get naked" stage. After what had happened at church the prior week, I felt I had good reason to be concerned. The band had practiced up at the church, and Casey went to the toddler room to play with Michaela, who was a year or so younger and the daughter of one of the band members. When we took a break, I went down to the toddler room to check on the girls. There they sat in two small rocking chairs, singing...with no clothes on. In a stern voice, I commanded them to get dressed, and although I dreaded hearing the answer, I asked, "Whose idea was this to take off all your clothes?"

Casey promptly confessed, "It was my idea, Mommy. Adam and Eve were naked in the garden, so I thought we would play Adam and Eve."

"Casey, we don't take our clothes off in public."

"What's public, Mommy?"

Hmm…I thought about how else I could get the point across. "Casey, we don't take our clothes off in front of other people."

"Of course we do, Mommy. I take my clothes off in front of the doctor, in front of Nana, in front of you, in front of Aunt Ter Ter…"

Finally, I left it at, "We *don't* take our clothes off at church!" That seemed to finally sink in.

*****

Summer passed quickly, and the heat of August in Nevada was intense that year. We started the day by going to the tennis courts. Casey played with some of the other children while I sweated profusely on the court, playing singles. Afterward, we went with Aunt Ter Ter to the hardware store to pick out a couple of plants to take to a housewarming party. My good friend and bandmate, Anita, had moved into her newly built house and had worked hard to do some landscaping during the past six weeks. She had planted flower seeds and was waiting impatiently for them to pop up out of the ground. I had planned to surprise her with some actual plants that she could see!

Casey went with Ter Ter to look for an extension cord she needed, and I went to look at plants. After picking out some flowering plants, I snuck up on the two of them in the store, surprising Casey. She squealed with delight. "Mommy, I didn't hear you coming. But most of all, I didn't smell you coming."

I wasn't quite sure what to say. "You can smell me?"

"Well, of course, Mommy, you sweated a lot, and we can all smell you, right, Aunt Ter Ter?"

Terry just walked off.

That comment forced the decision. We went home before going to Anita's so that I could shower and not smell. It was still sweltering hot, and I dressed in a tank top and shorts. We climbed into the car with the two plants and headed out.

As we were driving, Casey was staring at me intently. I looked over at her and asked, "What are you looking at?"

"Well, Mom, I'm just wondering. Nana said your freckles are angel kisses. I'm just wondering why the angels had to like you so much to kiss you that many times. You don't think they'll kiss me that many times, do you? I'm not sure I want them to like me *that* much!"

I assured her they would not and kept driving. When we arrived at Anita's, we presented her with the two plants to add to her landscaping project. Anita and I sat talking in the kitchen while Michaela and Casey went out to play in the yard. Anita was so excited as she told me one of her flowers had finally popped up from seed. She felt like a true gardener, growing flowers from seeds. Just as she was about to take me outside to show off her flower, Casey came running in the house.

"Anita, look! I picked you a flower!"

Uh-oh! That's right…Casey had picked Anita's only flower, the prize of her garden. Anita was so sad. I felt so badly. I had no idea what to say. I apologized, and we took off for home. I hoped the plants we brought her made up for the disappointment, even if just a little.

*****

Summer led to autumn, and we had an unexpected early snowfall that year. I had parked the car in the driveway the night before because of a garage sale I was planning. All sorts of items were spread out in the garage for tagging and organizing. The snow was piling up, and over a foot had accumulated by late afternoon. Samuel had come over to play with Casey, and I was cleaning house. The kids seemed to be doing fine playing in the living room, so I thought it safe to take a shower. After drying my hair, I noticed the house was far too quiet which, as a parent, immediately set off alarm bells. I searched the house for them, but they were not to be found. I ran out to the backyard; no one's there either. I bundled up and headed out the front door, hoping to find them. Much to my surprise and with great ingenuity, they had placed two planks of wood slanting down from the front hood of my car. The two of them had packed snow on the planks, and as I headed toward them, Casey was on her sled on the hood of my car, heading down the windshield and down the ramp. I was one *mad* mommy! Of course, Casey said it was Samuel's idea. He merely looked goon-eyed at her as usual and nodded. I'm not so sure it was his idea, but the two of them rarely saw me angry. They figured few words were probably best.

The next evening, Samuel called Casey on the phone to ask if she could come over to play. I heard Casey respond, "No, I can't come over. I have a date tonight." She then hung up.

When I asked her what that was all about, she told me in a matter-of-fact voice, "He made you mad yesterday, Mommy, so I decided I shouldn't see him today."

"But did you need to tell a lie? You don't have a date."

"Of course I do, Mommy. I have a date with you! Now what shall we do?" she asked.

*****

Christmas was upon us before we knew it. We were once again very busy with concerts and parties. We drove to the mountains with Jason to pick out and cut down our own tree. Jason had purchased a permit for us to cut a tree up in the mountains. So we set off in his pickup truck in search of the perfect Christmas tree. We spent a couple of hours, looking for the perfect tree, tromping through the snowy woods. When we finally spotted it, Jason chopped it down, and we loaded it into the back of his truck and headed back down the mountain toward home. We had not driven more than ten miles before we were pulled over by the police. The trooper asked to see the permit for our tree, but Jason had forgotten it at the house. Although we pleaded with the trooper, he still wrote Jason a ticket for a hundred dollars. That was one very *expensive* Christmas tree! And to make it worse, when we got home, we discovered that trees look a lot smaller outdoors than when you try to get them in the house! We had to butcher that tree to make it fit in the corner of our small living room!

We even had a caroling party at our house that year. About twenty-five friends came over and off we went in the neighborhood to sing carols at neighbors' doors. Casey would run up and ring the doorbell. Then we would all burst into song. Casey called it "Jammin' for Jesus" because everyone was required to wear "jam" pants. That was our term for the big baggie pants that weight lifters often wore that were popular at that time. When everyone was sufficiently freezing cold, we came back home and had chili and birthday cake for Jesus. It was a great evening!

The Christmas season was crazy busy as usual. I made it a big deal at our house for Casey. It was always one of my favorite holidays! I had very few memories of Christmas when I was growing up. There was one Christmas I remembered when I was small, and we were living at my grandmother's house. Momma had to put a rope down on the floor to divide what Santa had brought me and my brother. I wanted all the same types of things my brother did—a glove, a basketball, etc. The floor was labeled "Anne" on one side and "Gary" on the other. I vividly remembered the rope as I envied what was on the other side.

We never had a lot of extra things growing up, and Christmas day was usually fairly lean on presents. But our expectations were not high, so rarely were we disappointed. Christmas generally came and went without much fanfare when I was a child, but it was always a time for family. Uncles and aunts and cousins visited. It was time to reunite with everyone each year.

And I kept up that tradition. Even as an adult, I never missed going home for Christmas while my mother was alive. It was a hard and long lesson for me over the years to learn (and accept) that the gifts really didn't matter. My feelings were always seemingly being hurt at this time of year. I had always "accused" my mother of loving my brother more than me. As I grew older, the incongruence in value of gifts to my brother and I seemed to loom greater. One Christmas, he and his wife received a refrigerator freezer. I got an acrylic sweater. Another Christmas, he got a large check. I received a Timex watch with some rhinestones on it. I tried to politely tell Momma she could take the watch back and get a refund since I already had a very nice watch. She very politely responded that she couldn't take it back because she had bought it on a closeout sale. I left the watch there with my mother when I went back home, and it was still in the drawer when she died. We found it when we were cleaning out things, and my aunt finally took the watch, claiming it was hers!

I think I had watched too many movies growing up and longed for the nostalgia of that "perfect family time." I had always dreamed of white Christmases, lots of presents, the decorated house, lights on the outside, a large Christmas tree, caroling, reading the Christmas story, going to church on Christmas Eve, concerts, going to the Nutcracker, a birthday party for Jesus, and having lots of friends and family over. I was certain that I spoiled Casey on Christmas from the first one onward. We did all of those things, and we always looked forward to the holiday season. Yes, it was overboard, but it was always great fun! Each year, we lived out my dreams for the whole month of December and looked forward to it coming again during the other eleven months!

This particular Christmas, Uncle Gary and Aunt Susan were coming in to visit the day after Christmas. And Aunt Mary, my mom's only sister, was flying in from Florida on Christmas night. Since Aunt Mary loved to gamble, it was several days of casinos, eating, visiting, and sightseeing. For Casey and me, it was a very special Christmas to have blood family at our house. For years to come, we would be unable to travel at Christmas due to Casey's gymnastics schedule. Her competitive season always started right after Christmas, and Casey's coaches rarely let the gymnasts off for more than two days at a time. There was generally one week off practice in the summer, but during Christmas season, they were in high gear preparing for the months of competition that started in early January each year. That was the one sad thing about most Christmas seasons…my brother and his family were separated from us by a whole continent. Gary has always been a very special person to Casey. Being one of the few and constant male influences in her life, her love for him was palpable. His visit made that Christmas even more special.

Casey, Aunt Mary, and I took Gary and Susan back to the airport December 30. Aunt Mary was going to stay another five days. Casey always missed Gary terribly when they parted. It was no different this day when on the drive home, Casey sadly stated, "Mommy,

I wish Uncle Gary could have stayed, and we put Aunt Mary on the plane."

I felt terrible for Aunt Mary, who was sitting in the car with us and heard every word, but I think it put a spark of competition in her. For the next few days, Aunt Mary played nonstop with Casey, letting her win at Hungry Hippos and teaching her to weave on her new stitch pattern. After those next few days, Casey was sold on Aunt Mary and cried when we finally took her to the airport. Hopefully, those tears made up for the original slight Aunt Mary endured on the previous trip from the airport!

*****

That school year, I did some part-time teaching at a rather elite private school, teaching French to grades kindergarten through sixth. The school graciously allowed me to bring Casey on the days I worked, and she stayed in the kindergarten room during the hours I was busy. By the end of January, four boys had asked Casey to marry them, and six parents had called me to tell me their sons had crushes on her.

Casey was notoriously slow in getting ready to go places. She was meticulous in her appearance, some days changing clothes several times. Each day I worked, I prodded her to hurry. "Casey, please hurry! I cannot be late, or I'll get fired."

"What's fired, Mommy? Will they burn you to punish you, and will we have to call the firemen?"

"No, honey, it means they may tell Mommy to never come back to work again because I was late."

On the way home from school one day, Casey informed me, "Mommy, I really like it here, and I had a very good day. And guess what? They didn't even fire me or you today! And, Mommy, they think my last name is the same as yours. Why would they think that?"

"Well, usually children have the same last name as their parents. You have your dad's last name. I never changed my name when I got married. Do you remember when we talked about this earlier? But when you get married, you can change your last name to your husband's if you like."

"I might like that," she added thoughtfully. "But only if it's a good last name. I don't want it to be something stupid like Casey Basey or Casey Goat or Casey Foot."

"Or if you'd like, we *could* change your last name to my last name."

"Oh no, Mommy, my name is Casey Elizabeth McGranahan Jr., and I'll be that way until I decide if I want to get married and take that new name."

Casey had always been called a junior because she was the spitting image of her dad. Everyone who met her kept saying that if she had been a boy, she would have *had* to be a junior. So she became known as Casey Elizabeth McGranahan Jr. in her own mind.

The rest of the way home, I was grilled on what her last name would be if she married Samuel, Randy (the next-door neighbor who was at least sixty-eight), Nana's son, Brian, and just about every other boy she knew. Finally, she said, "What would my last name be if I married London?"

Really? The dog? Well, it *was* Valentine's week, and I guess she just had it on the brain.

She filled out Valentine cards for each of the children in her kindergarten class. She then cut out paper hearts and hid them all over the house. I continued to find those paper hearts months later. For Valentine's Day dinner, we went out to celebrate. She insisted on wearing her skates out to dinner. (Once again, we pick and choose our battles.) That night, I'm pretty certain she was the only person in the restaurant with skates on her feet!

Chapter 19

In March, Casey was nearing her fifth birthday. The year had flown by, and over the course of the year, she had determined she would grow up to be a cheerleader, then a firefighter, then a cheerleader (again), a singer, and finally a gymnast. She had learned her numbers and letters and could read and write many words. She had learned to whistle, steer a car, and make a ceramic bowl in pottery class. It was now time for the new round of birthday parties. And Casey was not disappointed.

After the third party during the week of her birthday, she lay exhausted on her bed. She was staring up at the ceiling and was finally quiet for the day. I plopped down on the bed next to her and thought she would be asleep within a minute, but she suddenly turned to me lying next to her and asked, "Mommy, will we be naked in heaven? And do you think we'll be able to see each other?"

I replied, "Well, the Bible indicates that we will all get new bodies in heaven, and that we will rejoice. So we probably won't care if we're naked, but I feel sure we'll be able to see and recognize each other from what the Bible says."

"That's good, Mommy. My Sunday school teacher told us there would be a party in heaven. And I just want to make sure that I'm going to know the people at the party. But I'm not so sure I want to be naked at the party."

The thoughts that ran through that child's head never ceased to amaze me! But the good news was that maybe she was over the "getting naked" stage once and for all!

Casey's mind and body continued to develop rapidly. By early April of that year, she was riding her bike without training wheels and doing "wheelies" off the curb. She could now jump rope forward and backward and could hit tennis balls back and forth for a ten-ball rally at times. In gymnastics, she had mastered cartwheels, handstands, and back walkovers.

Tact, however, was not an attribute she had developed yet. But her ability to use logic and intellect continued to entertain me. I had recently started dating a guy from church. It took Casey a while to warm up to him, but once she did, it was full speed ahead. Paul read to her, took her to lunch, played with her, and if he was there when she went to bed at night, he even took part in our prayer time.

One evening, as we were saying prayers, Casey left no doubt about what her feelings were. "And, God...I pray for a new daddy." I opened my eyes and looked at her. She opened her eyes and looked at me and then looked straight at Paul who still had his eyes closed and said *very* loudly, "And, God, bring him soon!"

The next Monday morning, Casey and I woke up to a stormy day. I opened the garage door to take the garbage out by the curb, and just at that time, the electricity went off. We had to finish getting ready and eat breakfast without electricity. By the time we got ready to leave for school, somehow it had slipped my mind that the electricity was off. We quickly loaded up the car, and I backed out into the driveway. I sat there for about two minutes, clicking the garage door closer and couldn't get the door to close. Casey sat there quietly as I got more and more frustrated. I finally realized that I needed to calm down. So I took a big breath, looked over at Casey, and tried to ask as lightheartedly as possible, "Casey...what do *you* think is wrong with this thing?"

She calmly looked over at me and replied, "Well, Mommy, does the garage door use electricity? Because if it does, the electricity is out." Boy, was I embarrassed!

*****

Age five was an adventure and deeper lessons were learned that summer. She learned that friendships can be fickle. She learned that children can be mean and cruel, and that Mommy is maybe the safest human on earth for her. After one friend chose to inform Casey that she preferred to play with Jenny because Jenny was more fun, Casey solemnly came in the house with tears in her eyes, saying, "Mommy, it sure does hurt when your heart gets hurt." Unfortunately, that is a lesson we never stop learning.

But on a lighter note, at age five, she learned to blow bubbles with her own spit, how to tie her own shoes, how to make spitballs and shoot them through a straw, how to play ping-pong and bingo, and how to cut herself some bangs (without my knowledge)! It was a magical summer of travel, swimming, gymnastics, and playtimes. She made me breakfast in bed several times—muffins, orange juice, and cereal. We visited dinosaur exhibits, went to county fairs, and watched fireworks and balloon races. We hiked in the mountains, went boating, flew to North Carolina, and she had her first real gymnastics event.

She was so excited. She only had a small part in the special presentation, but to her, it was a major event. She had to do a split jump and then go down into the splits on the floor after landing. She called Grandma and Grandpa to make sure they were coming. Grandpa told her they might be a little late because he had to shave so he could look good for the show. But Casey impatiently responded, "That's okay, Grandpa, you don't have to do that. Mom comes to gymnastics looking bad all the time." Yup…made me feel *real* good!

*****

By midsummer, Casey was in charge of doing numerous chores around the house. So I increased her allowance to ten dimes a week. She made her bed, put dishes away from the dishwasher, picked her room up, fed the dog, helped pick weeds and harvest the garden, and swept the deck. She continued to put nine dimes in her regular bank and one dime a week in her tithing bank. She always got her allowance on a Friday. She and Aunt Ter Ter really enjoyed going to garage sales on Saturdays. So Casey would save up her money and empty it out to go "garage saling" on nice Saturdays.

One Friday, as she was putting her dime in the tithe bank, she stood there staring at the bank thoughtfully. Finally, she said, "Mommy, does Jesus come down on Sunday and get the money out of the tithe bank? If so, he only takes some because there's still money in there each week. I shake it, and I can tell."

I explained that it was money we set aside for God's use. We had neglected to use it in the past for anything. It had just been sitting in that piggy bank. After we discussed it, the decision was made to empty the bank the last Sunday of each month and take it to church to put it in the offering box. The first time she dropped that money in the offering box, it brought tears to my eyes. There was no hesitation. She was delighted to give it. It was a lesson for me in the joy of giving!

Later that summer, I had read Casey the Bible story of Jonathan's son, Mephibosheth, who was born with two crippled feet. All week long, we continued to talk about Mephibosheth and played word games with his name to help her remember it. We read about how King David looked after him when his father died, even into his manhood. This story touched Casey deeply. Not only had he lost his father when he was a child (just like her), but he was also crippled. We discussed that no matter how bad we think we have it, there are always people who have it worse.

That next Sunday, as serendipity would have it, Casey's Sunday school lesson was also on Mephibosheth. The teacher began to talk about Jonathan's son and asked if anyone knew his name. Casey spoke right up and answered. The teacher told me after class that she was astounded, as most adults do not even remember the name (much less know how to pronounce it). As a proud Momma, I just said, "Yeah, she's pretty special!" (No, I did not tell the teacher we had been talking about him all week!)

Casey was very excited to tell me about the lesson at church. She was also excited to inform me, "Mommy, did you know that God has a very special place in his heart for widows and orphans?"

I assured her I did know that and told her how very blessed we were, much more so than some families. She made the suggestion that we adopt an orphan to support so that we could be like God and have a heart for orphans. So we did. We signed up to support a child in El Salvador. With my help, Casey wrote to him monthly. He wrote back several times and sent pictures. We posted the picture of Guillermo on the refrigerator and prayed for him daily. We supported him for six years until he was eighteen and never regretted a dime of it.

*****

As the summer drew to an end, I registered Casey for kindergarten. It was a bittersweet moment. I was very excited to have her start school, but she was growing up far too quickly for me. We decided to use the last two weeks before school started to make crafts for Christmas. We drove up to Lake Tahoe and collected pine cones, bringing them home to spray paint, adding glitter and ribbon with which to hang them. We made little gift boxes that were painted and decorated, and we sewed Christmas stockings with different colors of thread. We visited the ceramic shop, and Casey made bowls and cups. It was my last few weeks with her all to myself, the last few weeks of true childhood.

On the last Friday, before school started, I took Casey over to meet her teacher for initial testing. The teacher allowed me to stay in the room during testing which included building things with blocks, writing her name, drawing pictures, word association, and coordination skills. The last series of questions involved a scenario where Casey was to imagine she was lost. The teacher asked her if she could tell her the address where she lived, her telephone number, her full name, and her mother's name.

Casey promptly responded with the full address and phone number. She could actually write the address from having done it so many times on our envelopes to Guillermo. When the teacher prompted her for her full name, she proudly stated, "Casey Elizabeth McGranahan Jr."

The teacher looked over at me with questioning eyes and said, "Really?"

I tried to explain where this came from, and the teacher looked at Casey in a patronizing manner to say, "So your real name is Casey Elizabeth McGranahan."

But Casey stubbornly jutted her chin out and responded, "No, my name is Casey Elizabeth McGranahan Jr. And if you don't like that, then I'm not sure you can be my teacher!"

The teacher merely smiled and decided in a matter of nanoseconds that it wasn't a battle she wanted to fight. She continued on, "Do you know your mother's full name?"

"Yes, it's Elizabeth Anne Hope."

"Very good. Can you spell it?"

"Of course I can! M-O-M!"

And that concluded the interview and testing!

The next day, Casey lost her first tooth. She was so excited! We were attending a birthday party at the park when Casey came running up with blood dripping down her chin and a bloody smile. "Mommy, look! I did it! I lost my tooth." She held out her hand with the small tooth. "Here it is, but there's lots of blood." I kissed her right on the bloody mouth and told her how proud I was of her. She talked about losing that tooth for a whole month…until she lost a second one!

That next Monday, I took Casey to her first day of school. I took pictures of her walking up the steps and had tears in my eyes. She was very excited to go in and was not the least bit nervous. She looked up at me and said, "Mommy, it will be okay. You'll be fine. I'll be home in a few hours. And if it makes you feel better, you can come in with me to meet some of the kids."

I told her I would like that a lot. We went to her classroom, and I waited as the teacher helped her find her chair. As she was getting settled into her desk, putting supplies away, one little boy yelled out across the room, "Hey, are you her grandmother?" Geez…I was only thirty-three years old! Give me a break, kid! That took care of the tears. I wanted to reach over and grab the kid by his scruffy little neck.

But Casey came to my rescue. "Of course not, silly, that's my mom. My grandma is a lot older than that!"

It was definitely time for me to go!

Casey adjusted well to school. She really enjoyed being social, and she loved learning new things. By the end of the first week, she was nagging me to ride the bus to and from school. I inquired at the office to see if the bus went to our neighborhood. They assured me it did and told me that her teacher would walk her to the bus line that afternoon. She could ride the bus home from school that very day if she wished. So it was decided!

There I sat at the appointed hour, waiting for the bus. And I waited. I was getting more panicked by the minute. I had heard stories about kindergartners who rode the bus and got off at the wrong stop. After waiting almost an hour, I rode over to the school and ran to the office. There sat Casey sucking on a Popsicle. The principal came out and told me that a mistake had been made. The bus does not go to our neighborhood any longer because we were too close to the school. So Casey had stood in line until she was the only person left. The attending teacher brought her back into the office and tried to call me, but I, of course, was waiting at the bus stop. Since no one had cell phones at that time, I couldn't be reached. By the time I arrived, Casey was over the disappointment of not being able to ride the bus and was just happy to have a Popsicle. We were both ready to get home!

As the weeks flew by, her vocabulary increased rapidly. She had new spelling words and writing assignments each week at school. We started visiting the public library and would spend hours there each week, picking out new books to take home and read. She became fixated on Japan, and for weeks, we read new books on their culture, the land, and their history.

Each night at bedtime, we continued to read a Bible story and a regular book. I would lie next to her and rub her back until she fell asleep. I knew I would not be able to do that for much longer, so I cherished each night. Before long, she would want to read her own books. She would be too big for me to lie beside her and rub her back. So many nights I laid there listening to her breathe deeply in her sleep and wondered how I could be so fortunate. I loved this child beyond my wildest dreams! It was awesome to think that if I loved her *this* much, how much more God must love us. It was incomprehensible!

She was also my best friend. As I laid there, I knew that too would eventually change as she grew up. I would have to get use to that idea. But right at that moment, the thought made me sad. It would be hard. She was every joy I could imagine wrapped up into a precious bundle. I was also pretty sure that particular thought couldn't possibly be very healthy. I wondered how Abraham could have had the courage and willingness to take Isaac up the mountain to be sacrificed. I prayed that God would never ask such a task of me. I wasn't sure I could make it without her. She continued to be my lifeline. Somehow, I knew I would need to become healthy enough to be willing to give her up if that was what was asked. Eventually, she would grow up and separate from me. I was so hoping that it would be a gradual process, less painful than the anxious thoughts I had that night. As I drifted off to sleep, I imagined the possibility of the horrible teenage years that might come where perhaps I would be happy to separate myself! Ha!

*****

That fall, Casey continued to improve her gymnastic skills. Within a few short weeks, she lost several of her baby teeth and had gaping holes in her mouth. By the week of Halloween, she looked like a jack-o'-lantern and was beginning to catch a bad cold. On Halloween night, she had a raging fever from strep throat. It was a brutal night. I answered the door with trick-or-treaters, and Casey was dressed up as a sick girl in pajamas! Right in the middle of the heaviest traffic, Casey came running out of the bathroom with a tooth hanging by a thread from her mouth. She had been in the bathroom trying to pull the loose tooth out and was now crying. "Mommy, Mommy, I think I broke my gum."

She had a bloody mouth, and the tooth was hanging limply from her upper gum. I was trying not to laugh because it was apparent she was in pain. Some of the nerve endings were still quite sensitive, so every time she breathed in air, it hurt. The harder she cried, the more it hurt. I finished up with the astounded children at the door (who probably thought I was torturing my child) and ran to the bathroom for *Chloraseptic*. I quickly sprayed some on the gum to numb the area and yanked the tooth out. That seemed to take care of the momentary crisis.

After the foot traffic ceased for the night, I tried to get Casey to take some cold medicine to help relieve her congestion. She resisted emphatically, saying, "No, Mommy, it will make me throw up."

"No, it won't," I replied. We mothers knew those words were one of the oldest lines in the book for children who did not want to take their medicine. We argued for a bit, but finally I got stern and insisted, but I had no time to feel satisfied with my victory. She swallowed the second teaspoon of medicine and promptly threw up, not just the medicine but dinner and all. And she kept throwing up. It was all over her, the bed, and the floor.

As soon as she could catch her breath, she looked up at me with these big blue eyes, brimming with tears and said, "Mommy, you aren't mad at me, are you?"

It was heartbreaking and much, much worse than someone saying, "I told you so!"

*****

Fall folded quickly into the holiday season, which was the busiest time at our house. Casey was the "kinderbear" at her school for a week, meaning she was the "special" child all week. She was allowed to do show-and-tell each day of the week and share her interests, her family, and snacks. So each night, I baked new treats. On the first day, she shared pictures of her family and showed her latest tooth that fell out. On the second day, she told me she was sharing more family photos. But in reality, she and Aunt Ter Ter conspired to share one of my CDs with the class, inviting in other classes and even the principal. I was a bit embarrassed over that one.

Wednesday, she took Baby Amy to school and showed a wreath that we had made out of pinecones we collected from Lake Tahoe. It was confirmed…Baby Amy was definitely the ugliest doll ever. When I picked Casey up that day, her teacher laughed and made a point to tell me her low opinion of poor Amy's looks. On Thursday, Casey took a book on Japan to share with the class. She shared everything she had learned about Japan and expressed how much she wanted to visit there someday. Friday, she took a homemade "stained glass window" that we had made by pressing fall leaves and crayon shavings between two pieces of wax paper. She also took the tape and book, *The Little Engine That Could,* and the class listened to the tape while she turned the pages. All in all, by the end of the week, I realized just how much this child enjoyed being in the spotlight! No fear! No trepidation!

I was back in the studio, wrapping up a new recording project that fall, and it was election time in the country. For some reason, Casey was totally engrossed in the presidential election. The advertisements were prolific on television, and she had taken an interest. She would gladly give her opinion to each adult she encountered, emphatically stating that each should vote for Bush.

On one of the campaign ads, there was a discussion of how Clinton was proabortion. Casey asked me to explain what abortion was. I tried to explain the process, telling her that it was basically killing babies while they were still in the mommies' tummies. She was horrified, and from then on, she had a discourse for all adults who would listen.

"Are you voting? I hope so. You need to vote for President Bush! And make sure you *don't* vote for Bill Clinton. He thinks it's okay to cut the heads off babies while they are in their mommies' bellies and throw them away!"

On Election Day, she got up bright and early to watch the results. She watched most of the day until it was clear that Clinton would beat Bush. She was sorely disappointed and walked in the kitchen, stating, "Mommy, you need to stop what you're doing right now. I think Mr. Clinton won, and we need to stop and pray for our country right now!" Ah, the wisdom of babes!

*****

The holiday season rolled in, and we continued at our usual hectic pace. Every Thursday, Paul took Casey on a "date night." They would go out roller skating, ice-skating, sledding, to the movies, golfing, out to dinner, etc. I was usually rehearsing those nights. I had an extremely crowded schedule that season with the new recording project coming out. Fitting Christmas shopping into the schedule was difficult. So I was glad to hear Casey come bounding in and announce after one of her and Aunt Ter Ter's Saturday morning garage sale sprees, "Mommy, I got Uncle Gary's Christmas present, and he's going to *love* it. I found him a book at a garage sale on his favorite band. He's really going to like my present!"

My brother had always had a love affair with the Beatles. He had every recording they ever made, as well as original artwork, books about them, and memorabilia. I was thinking to myself that he probably already had the book that Casey had found, but I didn't want to burst her bubble. She pulled it out of her canvas bag that she took on her garage forages. There it was…a book on the Bee Gees! I laughed so hard I thought I would cry. Casey, of course, had no idea why I was laughing. I couldn't break her heart by telling her that was *not* one of his favorite bands. So I told her I was proud of her. We wrapped it and sent it to Uncle Gary for Christmas. Imagine his surprise when he opened his present to find a book on the Bee Gees, but he was a good sport and probably still has that book in his bookcase.

Our friends from Boise were visiting that Christmas in Lake Tahoe. Cathy and Pete came there every Christmas to visit her parents who lived in a wonderful chalet by the lake. This year, we were invited to come up and spend some time with them. What we thought would be a day trip wound up being a four-day trip. As soon as we drove the twenty-five minutes up the mountain, it began snowing. And it snowed more than six feet in the first ten hours. We were snowbound and had a wonderful time playing in the mountains.

But by the fourth day, our clothes were getting smelly, and we were getting a bit crazy from being cooped up. You can only build so many snow tunnels and snowmen! So that afternoon, we put on the snow chains and attempted to make it back down the mountain toward home. It took us four and a half hours to make what was usually a twenty-five-minute drive. As we neared the bottom of the mountain, one of the chains broke. I got out of the car to try and fix it, but the chain was wrapped around the axle. I didn't know what I was going to do. I walked back to the car to warm up before trying to untangle it again.

When I got in the car, Casey saw my distress and said, "It will be okay, Mommy. While you were out there, I said two prayers...one for you to be safe and one for the man who's coming to fix the car."

I looked at her quizzically and asked, "What man?"

"The man I prayed for to come."

No sooner had I opened the door to go back outside than a car pulled up behind us. Out jumped a man from his pickup truck and asked if I needed help. I was floored! He quickly untangled the chain. I got back in the car and looked intently at my daughter and said, "You're very weird...you know that?"

She just smiled and said, "Nope, Mommy, I'm fatherless, so God takes care of us!"

I almost cried. Instead I just gave her a big hug and told her how very, very special she was. The faith of children!

Chapter 20

Casey and I rang in the New Year at a small party held by a friend. Then we headed home right after midnight to begin the year. The weather had turned icy and freezing cold, so we stayed close to home for the next few days, except for a day of skiing. Both of us grew restless whenever we were cooped up for long periods of time. Casey was anxious for school and gymnastics to start again after the Christmas break. She had graduated from advanced beginners to intermediate level at gymnastics and couldn't wait to start her new class. She was the youngest and the smallest in the class. She had conquered the back walkover, and I just knew before long, she'd be doing double backflips! She was also reading now and had finished reading her first book that week (a Dr. Seuss book). I was so proud of her! All those nights of reading to her had seemingly paid off. She truly loved to read. She was happy with a book in her hand.

January passed quickly as we were both very busy. I was juggling three part-time jobs while Casey was at gymnastics or school. I taught biology at the community college, and Casey helped me grade papers...but only the multiple choice and true/false questions. No student ever complained that I had mismarked an answer. That was a testament to her meticulous work. Even at five years old, she hated to make mistakes. I continued to teach French at a private school and was also doing medical billing and coding for a doctor. It was a whirlwind, but we always looked forward to our evenings together. We would make trips to the library each week to pick up new books to read. *Hop on Pop, Green Eggs and Ham, You Look Funny,* and

Valentine's Day Grump were just a few that topped our philosophical reading list at night.

On Valentine's Day, Casey made me a wonderful card. Actually, it was a wish list with a "Happy Valentine's Day" and "I love you!" in it. She emphatically wrote that she was now wishing for a brother, a sister, and a dad! It used to be just a dad. Then it grew to be a dad and a brother. The request had now graduated to include a sister. I wondered years later at what point she came to accept that it just wasn't going to happen. I never knew exactly when, but by the time she was in middle school, she seemed a happy camper being an only child. As a teenager, she continually stated how she loved being an only child growing up. She learned to be grateful for all the opportunities she had experienced, many of which might not have been possible had there been multiple children in the family. In addition, I'm not so sure she would have wanted to share my attention with another child.

We visited Grandma and Grandpa later on Valentine's Day, and Casey received several new books from them. She couldn't wait to get started. She jumped up on Grandpa's lap and dug into the first book. Grandpa tried to help her figure out words phonetically, and it was pretty funny. For the most part, it worked. But as she came across the word *what*, she struggled. Grandpa was trying to assist her and really wanted her to figure it out on her own.

"Casey, what word do you see in those four letters that you already know?" Grandpa asked.

"Hat! I see it, Grandpa," she exclaimed. Then with exuberance and confidence, she yelled out *what*, which sounded nothing like the word but rhymed with hat.

A new lesson was learned…life is *full* of exceptions. We all had a good laugh. Even at that age, she had learned to laugh at herself. It would serve as one of her best qualities as she continued to grow and mature. I wished I had learned to laugh at myself at such a young age. It seemed to come naturally to her, not to take herself too seriously.

I went on a field trip with her kindergarten class to the fire station that next week. The fire chief gave the students a lesson in what to do in case of a fire. He repeated over and over, "Stop, drop, and roll," and asked if everyone understood what he meant. All heads nodded affirmatively. So he asked for a volunteer to demonstrate. Of course, Casey was the first and only child to raise her hand. She stepped forward proudly and began the demonstration. She stopped abruptly, dropped into a crouch, did a forward roll, and stood quickly, giving a gymnastics salute finish. Everyone burst out laughing, especially all the firemen in the room. Little did she know that she was supposed to stop, drop flat to the ground, and roll in a sausage roll. Everything was relative to gymnastics in Casey's world. At first, she was confused by the laughter and a tiny bit embarrassed, but she bounced back quickly and laughed along with everyone else in the end.

I tried to introduce a little diversity into her gymnastics obsession, and I started Casey in karate that winter. It soon became obvious that she takes after her mother. And as with anything, she dove into it full force. It was tough to get her out of her "gee," the white pajama uniform for karate. For the first few days, I let her sleep in it. Then enough was enough. It had to be washed! That weekend, she spent the night at Samuel's house and went to tae kwon do the next morning with him. She had her karate "gee" with her but had forgotten her belt. It was a crisis. Samuel's mom found a tie to a white bathrobe, and that worked just swell. Oh, to be able to find solutions that easily all the time!

Casey progressed rapidly in karate, earning belt after belt. Our lives became busier and busier. What started out as twice a week at gymnastics was now three times a week. With karate on the other two weekdays plus school, it was a hint of the pace of life to come in the years ahead. She was a determined child. She wanted to be good at everything! She practiced everything with a vengeance. With her flexibility from gymnastics, her karate kicks had become quite good, and she regularly practiced it on anyone who let her. Poor Paul... he endured many surprise kicks to the groin. At one point, it got so frequent I had to have a talk with her sensei. I'm not sure what he said to her, but the sensei put a stop to it, and there was never another problem.

Chapter 21

The first five years had come and gone so quickly! We celebrated Casey's sixth birthday in a relatively quiet fashion that year. We had a party at school for her and one at Grandma and Grandpa's. Life was very fun and very busy. Casey had her first singing debut at one of my Easter concerts in front of about eight hundred people. She didn't seem intimidated at all. In her Easter bonnet and dress, she stood there and just belted out, "I am just a little girl who can change the world, change the world, change the world. I am just a little girl who can change the world 'cause Jesus made a change in me!"

It brought tears to my eyes as I thought even then how very true those words were. She was unique and special. God had formed her in my womb, and against many odds, she was healthy! I reminded myself that God never makes mistakes or accidents. He already knew all her abilities, and he had given her all the gifts and talents she would ever need to complete the work that he desired her to do. It was an overwhelming thought to know that no one else will have all the same experiences she will have. No one else will interact with all the people she will have in her life. No one else is perfectly suited to fulfill God's purpose in her life. But ultimately, the choice would be hers.

It was an awe-inspiring Easter as I ruminated on those thoughts for most of the afternoon. Indeed, I knew beyond a shadow of a doubt that she would change the world. After all, each of us do. For good or for bad, we all have an effect on our world. Our choices in this life make a difference. God designed and equipped each of us to fulfill specific roles and purposes in his plan. I couldn't help but wonder what her callings in life would be. What purposes had God created her for. Would she make wise choices? The only thing I knew for sure was that it would be an adventure. A walk with God at the helm always is, and I felt in my heart that even at such a young age, she had definitely chosen to walk with God.

It was also comforting for me as a single mother to know that God was always in control, and I don't have to be. It was a lesson I hoped to continue to teach Casey as she grew older. Oh yes, there were times when I wanted to take control back and do it my way, but it was special that even at her young age, I felt I could share the good, the bad, and the ugly of actions and decisions with Casey. For each of us, the lessons learned brought us closer to an understanding of God's grace and unfailing love. We often discussed how God always sees his children through his eyes of love, forgiveness, and compassion.

Even later, many times, I reflected on those talks we had. I often reminded myself that even when I make poor choices, God always sees me as the person he made me to be with all the potential for which he created me. It has always been special for me to be able to share my faults and weaknesses over the years with Casey. Her love has been a "skin" example that taught me real truth and real trust. Her love made God's love even more real. Because of my love for her, I could understand so much better the depth of love God has for me. I could rest in the fact that *nothing* could separate me from his love. I could be assured that even though he knows everything about me, he still chooses to love me and use me. I was still his kid no matter what! I could rejoice that he wants to give me the desires of my heart, as well as the tools with which to fulfill those desires for his glory and his purpose.

It was so special to be able to share these thoughts with Casey, to reassure her of such a love, to make it real to her. I wanted her to know in her heart of hearts that no matter how we old become or how young we are, no matter what happens in our lives, God will continue to give us purpose and a wonderful anticipation of opportunities to come. That Easter, I knew more so than at any prior time that I wanted my daughter to always have that sense of adventure with God…that anything is possible through him…that he wants to give us the desires of our hearts, and that we don't have to be perfect or overachievers.

But I also wanted her to know that God is not merely a genie in a bottle. We read Scripture that talked about God's love. Then we read Scripture about God's holiness. We talked about how Jesus said, "If you love me, you will obey my commandments." Then we discussed what it meant to obey.

She astutely asked, "Mommy, when I don't obey you, does that mean I really don't love you? 'Cause I feel like I always love you!"

"Well, honey," I replied, "most likely you love *you* more at those times when you disobey me. You want to do something or say something out of line more because *you* feel like it. You aren't really thinking of loving me during those times, are you?"

"I guess not, but I'm always hoping you don't get too mad at me when I disobey. I don't like it when you put me in time out, and we're separated 'cause you're disappointed in me. But the good thing is this, Mommy, I know that when I say I'm sorry, you will always forgive me and hug me and tell me you love me."

I could not have put it into words any better! That's pretty much the way I feel each time I disobey God!

Chapter 22

After Easter, we took a break and spent a week in San Diego with a lady friend from church who owned a condo on the beach. Casey learned to roller blade at full speed on the boardwalk. I continued to learn to relax. We spent our days singing to the radio, roasting marshmallows on the beach, and playing in the surf. When we returned home, there were only a few weeks left to finish up the school year. The end-of-year program at Casey's school was a musical performed by all the kindergarten classes combined about the three little pigs and the big bad wolf. Casey adored pigs, so she was very excited about the musical. She always told me when she grew up, she was going to have a pig as a pet. (And she did!)

As the school year ended, I prepared for my trip to China. I was going on a short-term mission trip for three weeks. It would be my first long trip without Casey, and I was having real anxiety over it. It became a whirlwind of activity as I decided to put our house on the market at about the same time. Both of us were very excited about looking for a new house. We prayed about it each night.

I placed a "For Sale by Owner" sign in the front yard so that we could try to save money on a realtor's fee. On the first day the sign was placed in the yard, which was a Saturday, a man showed up at our door and asked to look at the house. He walked through and said very little. He appeared to be Indian or Pakistani, and his English was not very good. After less than ten minutes of looking through the house, he left, and I thought very little of it. He was our first looker, and we were in no real hurry.

Much to my surprise, less than two hours later, the man showed up again with his wife and two children, offering me the asking price with a cashier's check in his hand. I was flabbergasted! The only bad thing was that he wanted to move in within six weeks. For a few minutes, I panicked as I thought about my upcoming trip to China the next week. Then Casey looked up at me with her big blue eyes, with a smile as big as could be, and said, "God sure is good, isn't he, Mommy?"

It was a done deal. I accepted the check and completed the sale, having no idea where Casey and I would live after I returned from China. We started cleaning out closets, packing, and throwing things away. One afternoon, we cleaned out the cupboard in Casey's bathroom. There was so much junk in there, and I was amazed at how large it was after we cleaned it out. Casey exclaimed that it was large enough to sleep in and asked if she could sleep in there that night. I laughed and agreed, thinking by evening she would forget. But as bedtime drew near, she gathered up blankets and her stuffed animals and made herself a bed in the cupboard. With the light on and the cupboard door open, she went right to sleep. Oh, the joy of simple life experiences!

Casey was going to stay with our friends, the Maxwell's, while I was in China. We had less than two weeks to finish packing and find a new house for when I returned. And we had not yet begun to look at houses! I was so nervous about leaving her for that length of time. It appeared I was handling the anticipated separation worse than she was. I realized that her Kindergarten graduation would take place while I was in China and cried all night, knowing I would miss it. Grandpa, Aunt Ter Ter, and Jason promised to attend the graduation. Aunt Ter Ter assured me she would film it so that when I returned, we could have a "graduation watch party." I cherished that film; she looked so cute in her white cap and gown!

I called her twice from China. Calling internationally was not so easy back then. On the first time, it seemed that she missed me, and I was happy to be missed. The second time, she was in a rush and, after a few sentences, said, "Mommy, gotta go...we're going swimming at the lake. Talk to you later. Bye!"

She hung up the phone, leaving me devastated. Apparently the lake was more important, and she didn't want to talk more. I was *definitely* missing her more than she was missing me!

*****

China was a wonderful experience. I flew into Hong Kong where I would be based and took short flights over to China with suitcases full of Bibles. The only toiletries or change of clothing I had were stuffed into my backpack. It was illegal to smuggle Bibles into mainland China at that time. So prior to departure, I was given training on how to act, what to wear, where to meet up with the mainland missionaries, and what to do if I was caught going through customs. I knew I was in God's hands and had spent much time in prayer, yet on my first time entering China, I was petrified. Each of us was required to enter the country alone, not as a group, so as not to attract too much attention.

I flew alone from Hong Kong to Beijing. As I was standing in line to go through customs, I noticed there were guards at every scanning station armed with machine guns. Each and every piece of luggage was being scanned in the X-ray machine. I felt doomed and knew there was no way I could hide the fact that those were books in my suitcase. There was not a single article of clothing…only Bibles written in Chinese.

By the time it was my turn to go through, I felt like I was visibly shaking. All of a sudden, there was commotion to my right, and the guards from all stations near me ran over to where a group of Japanese tourists were trying to innocently bypass customs. The guards were yelling and shoving them with their rifles just as my luggage was going through the X-ray machine. The attendant was looking at the commotion, and my luggage passed through with no issues. I quickly grabbed my backpack and large suitcase off the belt and did my best to walk calmly to the exit while giving thanks and praise! I was totally amazed at how innovative God was at that moment!

I found my prearranged meeting place with the "undercover" missionary to make my delivery. After sharing a meal, we headed out to a local underground church meeting. It was an amazing time of song and worship. I couldn't understand a word of what was said or sung, but their fervent passion for God was palpable in the room. These churchgoers were literally risking their lives, and the lead pastor had recently been released after spending several years in prison for teaching Christianity. It humbled me to see their gratefulness, their hunger, and their passion for the Word. The excitement of having their very own Bible was visible on every face.

After the service, I shared a meal with the attendees. I sat in between the pastor and the missionary, who interpreted for me. After hearing details of his seventeen-year prison stay, I expressed my inability to comprehend how these people could choose to undergo such persecution each and every day.

I will never forget his reply as he smiled and said, "It is an honor to be persecuted for my Savior. The persecution we endure here has a purpose. Christianity is spreading quickly, and we are humbled to be a part of God's great plan. What I do not understand is how Americans choose to live under the constant veil of the persecution of disillusionment. They have the Gospel available to them, and they are free to worship whenever and wherever they wish, yet they continue to see little value in the precious gift they have been given. Instead, they live with the disillusionment that it is things that will satisfy them. So they accumulate, they hoard, they neglect to share what they have...perhaps not so much because they are selfish, but because they really believe these things are worthwhile and will make them happy and fulfill them. Personally, that would not be living to me. I prefer the type of persecution our people endure to the persecution of disillusionment."

I had no idea how to respond. The truth of those words stung me to the core. Here in front of me were people who were willing to risk it all for a treasure that was too precious to buy. And there I sat, representing a people who, with a futile effort, sought out treasures that had no lasting value, bombarded with propaganda each and every day that said, "Have it your way, because you are worth it, you deserve a break today." I knew that pastor was right. We have been indoctrinated with the idea that we need things to make us better, more attractive, more desirable, and more marketable. We have lost sight of the real treasure. I left that gathering with a sadness in my heart, desiring somehow to change this perception for my daughter, even if for no one else.

*****

The beauty of China was breathtaking. Beijing was in the northern province, and I was looking forward to touring the area after making my delivery. For the next three days, I was just a tourist. China was one of the most beautiful places I had ever seen. On the first day, I explored Beijing City, Tiananmen Square, Happy Valley, the Ming Tombs, and Temple of Heaven. I rode in rickshaws and marveled at all the cyclists in this crowded city. I was only uncomfortable when people were staring at me—which was most of the time. The Chinese people had been cloistered for so long under communism that most were unfamiliar with Westerners. Few people had seen blue eyes or freckles or blond hair. Several asked my interpreter if I had a skin disease. So I self-consciously purchased an extra shirt with long sleeves and a long skirt to cover my freckles, even though it was near one hundred degrees. People still stared at my hair and eyes, and more than once, children asked to touch my light-colored hair. I was a novelty for them.

On the third day of that first mainland visit, I had the incredible opportunity to visit the Great Wall of China. The most well-preserved areas of the wall were outside the city. It was one of the most awe-inspiring experiences I have ever had. The countryside was stunning, and its beauty made my heart swell with the awesomeness of nature that God had created. There was relatively little commercialism at that time in the area, and I was able to freely walk the wall as far as I wanted.

On the way back to the city, I stopped at a cloisonné factory. There I was able to do most of my souvenir shopping. But the most fascinating part of the stop was the two hours I spent watching the Chinese workers use their specialized technique to decorate metal objects, cloisonné.

I flew back to Hong Kong the next day to stock up on Bibles once again. My next trip to the mainland was three days later to the southern part of China. When it was time to fly into Guangzhou (also known as Canton), I was feeling less nervous. The airport was not nearly as large, but the guards at customs were just as armed and stoic. I felt certain I would make it through customs with no problem after my first experience. I had prayed less and worried less. But as the old saying goes, "Man plans, and God laughs."

Once again, I saw they were scanning every piece of luggage. As I drew closer to going through customs, I kept waiting for some distraction or commotion to occur. Yet to my horror, as my luggage passed through, the commotion actually became me. Guards surrounded me, pushed me with their rifles, and ushered me into an interrogation room with no windows. Two guards were present; one was screaming at me in Chinese, and the other guard merely pointed his rifle at me. I was trying to remain calm and told him I spoke no Chinese. A third guard brought in my suitcase, opened it up, and found the Bibles. He started throwing them at me across the room, continuing the tirade in Chinese. I had no idea what was being said, but I was certain it wasn't a welcome speech.

All the guards finally left the room, and I waited in the hot stuffy room surrounded by Bibles all over the floor, becoming more and more nervous. About two hours later, two different guards came in. One spoke broken English, and as he bent down to pick up one of the Bibles, he held it up and stated, "This book illegal. Why you bring in our country? Do you mean to propaganda our people? Who you see here in city? Who meet you to buy from you?"

I quickly prayed that God would give me the right words to say. I looked up at the man from my metal chair and said quietly, "This is a good book. It brings hope to people. I wanted to give these away to bring hope to your people. No one is buying them, and I am not meeting anyone."

I had no idea if he had understood me or not. He just snorted and replied, "Foolish woman! This is not lawful, and you can go to jail. No care if you are American."

He spoke again in Chinese to his companion, and the other officer left the room. The remaining guard stared at me for a very long time. Then without saying another word, he tucked a small Bible under his belt, covering it with his shirt. He didn't smile. He didn't talk. He just stared at me as if warning me not to speak. The other guard returned with a garbage sack and tossed all the remaining Bibles in the sack. Once all the books were confiscated, both guards left. I remained in that room for over twelve additional hours. It was so hot and stuffy; I was beginning to smell myself.

At last, a new set of guards came in. The only English that was spoken was simply, "You leave." They escorted me to the airline desk where an agent issued me a return flight to Hong Kong. The guards accompanied me to the boarding area and made sure I was on the plane. Everyone was staring. I was a criminal, but I was going back to freedom.

The only part of southern China I saw, other than the inside of the airport and an interrogation room, was from the window of the plane. And it was not a pretty sight. A major storm had passed through the area a few days prior to my arrival. It had been all over the news. Flooding had killed hundreds, wiped out crops, and had created mudslides. As we took off, the devastation was evident. Dead animals littered the streets. Mud was everywhere. Houses were leveled. I left China that day with a profound sense of sadness and with a prayer that the one book hidden in a guard's shirt would somehow bring hope to some. Somehow, God's Word had managed to get through, even if it didn't go as I planned!

My last few days were spent in Hong Kong where I transferred my remaining Bibles to a group who would later try to get them into China. My face was now known to border guards, so I would not be able to make any more border crossings. And by now, I was feeling very homesick for my child and was anxious to get home.

I had a concert in California coming up, so rather than go home, I flew into San Francisco where I was met by Casey and Aunt Ter Ter. As soon as I exited customs, there was my baby girl with balloons and flowers, running up to me and jumping in my arms. I was home; she *was* my home!

Chapter 23

When we finally returned home, it was a crazy time of packing up the house and looking for a new place to live. In between those two activities, Casey was busy learning to skid and leave rubber marks with her bike. It became obvious we would not be able to find a place to move into very quickly. I began to pray about what we would do in the interim. After a couple of days, my friend, Eileen, offered to let us move in with her for a couple of months. She had a two-story house, was a single parent, and her two children (although a bit older) played with Casey all the time. It was an ideal situation for us, and Casey was very excited.

Summer was in full bloom, and it was a lively, if not frantic, time. Ter Ter was getting married in September. Casey was to be the flower girl, and I would be singing, but we still managed to fit in some camping trips between all the activities. We took our ski boat to lakes, and I tried to teach Casey to water ski. She got up on two skis quite easily. But once up, she consistently had difficulty keeping the skis together. Gradually, her legs went into a split position until her bottom was dragging the water. Only then did she let go!

We continued to look at a seemingly endless number of houses. Neither of us liked the process much, but it was particularly distasteful to Casey. After all, that would mean moving away from Eileen's, which at the time was a dream come true. To her, she now had the brother and sister she had always wanted.

Each night, I continued to read the Bible with Casey and would follow that up by reading other books. Then most nights, I sang her to sleep. Eileen's children became part of our bedtime routine. They joined us for reading time, and we would all cuddle on Casey's bed in the "secret room," which was a playroom that we converted into a small bedroom. We all said prayers, and then Erick and Melissa went off to bed.

One evening, after singing Casey to sleep, Melissa tiptoed to my bedroom door and knocked quietly. I was still reading and told her to come in. She climbed up on the bed with me and said, "I'm having trouble sleeping tonight. Will you come sing me to sleep?" This too became part of our nightly ritual as long as we were there. Casey wasn't the only one in our family who enjoyed having brothers and sisters around!

By the end of summer, we had found a house, but we still had to wait several weeks for the house to close until we could move in. Casey would be going to a new school, and she was very nervous about moving into a new neighborhood with new children and a new school. To add to the trauma, I had recently been to the doctor about some moles on my face that had begun secreting liquid. The doctor stated they needed to come off, and come off soon!

The surgery was outpatient, and I was supposed to get a couple of stitches for each of the moles removed. It was to be simple surgery. When I woke, my whole face was bandaged, and I could barely move my mouth. I had no idea what had happened. The doctor came in and explained, "When I went in to remove the moles, I found they were connected by a tumor below the skin. I had to remove the whole tumor which required twenty-six stitches. I put the stitches in your smile line and did dermabrasion on your face to reduce the scarring. Basically, I removed the top layer of skin on your face to reduce the scarring. Unfortunately, your face will be a scab and covered with gauze for about a week, but I believe the tumor is benign."

I was shell-shocked, and I was in pain! Eileen picked me up from the outpatient clinic, and I looked like a bloody mummy. The scabs on my face oozed for a week, and it scared the children at first. But Casey grew accustomed to it quickly and, by the end of the day, was giving me a hug and kiss, setting off to go play. Even in the midst of preparing for a wedding, Aunt Ter Ter came over to Eileen's and helped care for both Casey and I the next few days. She tended to my bandages, washed my bloody pillowcases and sheets, and made sure Casey was bathed and fed. Her compassion and love for us was more than anyone could have asked.

A week later, I returned to the doctor. He removed all the bandages, and I cried. The long scar down my face would take some getting used to. Now I also knew what it was like to be physically scarred. Everywhere I went, people stared. The doctor assured me the scar would get less prominent with time, but I was skeptical. The left side of my face was distortedly swollen for months. The scar faded with time, but it would be a long time before I felt comfortable in public and no longer felt deformed.

Thankfully, there was too much to do to be totally consumed with my looks. We had to clean the new house, get new carpet, redo the kitchen, wallpaper, get Casey enrolled into a new school, and buy some more furniture. When we moved out of our previous house, the man who bought it also wanted to buy most of my furniture. Since I had no place to store it, I agreed. But now, I had to do some fast shopping. School was to start the next week, and we needed to get moved in.

*****

It was late August, and my birthday had rolled around yet again. Casey was spending the day with her cousin, and we were going to have dinner that evening. As I was waiting for Casey to return, I received a call from my father-in-law. Grandpa seemed to be sputtering, struggling to say what was on his mind. Finally, he broke down crying and said he had been diagnosed with lung cancer and had only about eight months to live at best. He begged me not to tell Casey, but I didn't think I could honor that request. Somehow, I just didn't think it was a fair request. Still, at the time, I told him I would think about it.

I had grown up very close to my grandmother. She had a profound effect on my life. She more than half raised me, and I had loved her with all my heart. I was about fourteen when she died. To me, it had seemed like a sudden death, and I felt like I never had the chance to say many of the things I had wanted to say. I was never told how ill she was. Even when they took her to the hospital, I always thought she would come home. The hospital was over thirty miles away, and I never got to visit her. When she died, I felt cheated and hurt. I had wanted to be with her, to comfort her, to know her even better. I had loved her so much…I didn't want Casey to feel the same way about her grandfather. So I knew I would probably figure out a way to tell her soon.

We moved into our new home, and Casey got situated in her new school, making new friends each day. The neighborhood was full of children who went to her school, and it was a blessing for her to have so many children to play with. Our house became the neighborhood "playhouse." We had a trampoline in the backyard, a basketball hoop, and Casey had a huge bedroom filled with all kinds of toys, including a small balance beam. There were sleepovers on most weekends when we weren't traveling for gymnastics or concerts. I had always wanted to have a houseful of children, so I loved every minute of it!

Casey started piano lessons that November and was thrilled to begin. She practiced excitedly each day…at least for the first year! Between school, gymnastics, piano, and friends, our schedule was overly full entering the holiday season. The time was drawing near to Thanksgiving, and I knew I needed to break the news to Casey about Grandpa soon. I was dreading it.

One evening, as we were kneeling for prayers, I told Casey we needed to pray for Grandpa…that he had lung cancer. She looked at me stricken.

"Is Grandpa going to die, Mommy?" she asked.

I didn't want to lie to her, so I told her the truth. "Yes, he probably will. He has incurable lung cancer, and he may not live a whole lot longer…maybe not even until summer."

Casey looked up at me with big tears in her eyes. "Mommy, does everyone who gets cancer die? Grandma Colvin died, daddy died, and now Grandpa…"

"Well, we all die at some point. But no, not everyone who gets cancer dies from cancer," I replied. "But it is a very bad disease that is difficult to treat."

We finished saying our prayers that night, praying that Grandpa would stop smoking, and that God would heal him if it was in his will. I laid with her for a long while that night trying to comfort her. Finally, she fell asleep. But in the middle of the night, she wandered into my bedroom and crawled in bed with me. I snuggled her close and asked her if she was okay. Her reply kept me awake the rest of the night.

"Mommy, I'm worried about Grandpa. I don't think he knows Jesus, and I need to do something about that!" Once again, Jesus's words rang true. We really should all become like little children. They see a problem, and they want to figure out a way to fix it if it's important to them, obstacles or not, fearless...determined. When did we as adults lose that? When did we become so afraid of rejection and worried about what others would think if we tried to witness?

For weeks, Casey was despondent, but she didn't cry again. I could tell she was still trying to process the information. She seemed to take solace in her piano playing. More than once, she stated, "Mommy, I just want to make sure that Grandpa really gets to hear me *really* play before he dies."

She seemed to have a knack for the piano and picked it up quite easily. By the end of November, she was playing her first songs and a few chords. Between school, gymnastics, karate, and piano, she kept very busy, but the sadness pervaded at night.

In late November, I met with her teacher for my first parent-teacher conference. Perhaps there is a bit of dread for every parent before one of these conferences. After all, I wasn't quite sure if I merely viewed my child through extremely rose-colored glasses. I was prepared for the worst, wondering what trouble and mischief she induced at school. But the teacher soon allayed my fears when she asked, "What's it like to have a perfect child who is kind, generous, respectful, and includes everyone?"

I was bursting with pride but could only reply, "Well, I think she's really trying to be like Jesus!" The teacher didn't quite know what to say, so we left it at that.

On my way home from the conference, I couldn't help but think of all the times Casey really was such a wonderful child. Just the previous night, she proved how very patient she was despite being so young. I had been watching my show (*ER*), which was my weekly ritual. Casey usually left me alone during that hour so that I could relax. That evening was no different, and she went upstairs to pick up her room, play a bit, and get ready for bed. Usually, she would call out to me when she was ready for prayers and reading. It had only been a short while, and she calmly called down, "Mommy? Mommy? Can you come?"

I replied, "I'm watching my show. I'll be up in a few minutes."

Another fifteen minutes went by, and she calmly called down again, "Mommy? Mommy? Can you come?"

I replied again, "Casey, I'm watching my show, and I'll be up in a few minutes."

It was very quiet upstairs, and I thought perhaps she was already in bed, reading some. But as soon as my show ended, she calmly called down again, "Mommy? Mommy? Can you come now?"

I rounded the corner from the den to go up the stairs to her bedroom and saw her sitting in the hall walkway upstairs. Her legs were dangling over the edge of the second-story floor, and her head was stuck between two of the metal slats in the railing. She couldn't move. I calmly asked her what she was doing there.

She replied, "I wanted to see if I could fit my head through the railings, and I did it, but now I can't get my head back out. I'm stuck, Mommy."

I couldn't help but laugh, but that was not the correct response! That only frustrated her and made her cry. "It's not funny, Mommy. I'm stuck and can't get out!"

She had patiently been waiting up there for over forty-five minutes for my show to end! I quickly climbed the stairs, trying to suppress the smile on my face. I stood behind her and turned her head sideways to try and slip it back through. I could not, for the life of me, figure out how she got her head through there in the first place. It was not about to budge through those metal slats again. I even tried using Vaseline to lubricate her head, hoping it would somehow slide through, but we had no success.

So at 10:00 p.m., I called Jason. He came over with a crowbar and pried the metal slats apart so that my precocious six-year-old could escape. She had sat in her "jail" for over ninety minutes, waiting patiently for the issue to be resolved. After her escape, she sat in my lap in the big stuffed chair in the den and fell asleep in my arms. As I sat there, the specialness of her washed over me anew.

Chapter 24

The holiday season was upon us again, our favorite time of year when we *always* made sure we threw a birthday party for Jesus—cake and all! From Thanksgiving to Christmas, we were nonstop with concerts, decorating the house, having people to dinner, a first piano recital, going to *The Nutcracker*, and baking.

Each Christmas season, we tried to do something special for someone else. This year, Casey's whole first-grade class went to a nearby nursing home and presented a Christmas musical for the residents. Their young faces radiated joy! The magic of Christmas was shared with these lonely people through the eyes of children. It was a great evening. The children sat in the laps or at the feet of the older adults as they told them what they were hoping to get for Christmas. The conversations were simply magical. On the way home, I discussed with Casey how much it meant to "give" that time to those adults. It was a gift where nothing was expected in return. We discussed how Scripture tells us it is better to give than to receive and how we can be blessed so much by giving to others.

Casey surprised me by replying, "Mommy, I got a lot from tonight! I liked giving our program to those people. And I liked sitting there talking with them. But what I liked most was when they would get these big tears in their eyes when I asked them what they were hoping to get for Christmas. Do you know what almost all of them said? They were hoping some family would come visit them. I realized how lucky I am to have you there with me every Christmas, every holiday. Mommy, we might be a small family, but it's important, and it's special, and we have lots of people who love us and treat us like family, so we are very lucky."

I agreed with her, barely getting the choked-up words out of my mouth. These wise words from the heart of a child were my very own Christmas present.

*****

The new year continued to bustle with activity. Between gymnastics, karate, piano lessons and practices, and school, we worked in snow skiing, golf, trips to the library, visits with friends and family, and boys! That's right! Boys had begun to call consistently. Not just one or two but eleven or twelve each week. It was crazy! I would hand her the phone, and she would giggle a bit and hang up after about a minute. So I didn't worry too much about it at the time. After all, she had just lost a front tooth and had a gaping hole in the middle of her mouth. It was hard to take it too seriously!

A couple of weeks later, however, I began to notice that each day, when I picked her up from school, she had grass in her long hair, as well as dirt and grass stains on her clothes. I asked if they were doing some new outdoor activities in school, but she openly replied, "No, the boys are trying to kiss me, and they chase me until I fall down. But they eventually get the kiss, and then they help me back up."

I wasn't sure how to respond to that. It was one of the few times I had no come back! I thought about it all the way home.

After I turned the car off, I turned to look at her and asked, "Casey, they don't hurt you, do they?"

She started laughing. "Oh, Mommy, you're so funny. They couldn't catch me unless I let them. And if they tried to hurt me, they'd be *real* sorry! I know karate!" She grinned her goofy smile with the gaping hole and stuck her tongue through it, laughing as she got out of the car!

Before long, it was Valentine's Day. Casey made homemade cards for everyone in her class and printed them off the computer. We bought a bag of heart candy, and she painstakingly picked out the exact heart she wanted to give each person in their card. The words had to be just right for the person. "You're sweet, love you, be mine, cute, you're okay, nice, my pal, etc." During the more than two hours it took to do this Valentine chore, I contemplated if I could make money by starting my own brand of Valentine candy hearts with short sayings that adults could give out on Valentine's Day while working or doing errands. My imagination took off, and I thought about how I would coyly place one on a grocery cart or the table at a restaurant I was walking by or on the desk of a coworker. I could picture the person reading the Valentine heart. "Be nice. Think about it. Think again. Don't even think about it. Don't worry. Be useful. Stop! Leave. Pray about it. Someone is watching. Fight fair." Yup, I was certain I could make money!

Chapter 25

March came all too soon, and Casey turned seven. The years continued to pass all too quickly. It was a wonderful adventure. Each stage of her life brought new challenges and new lessons to be learned. She had lost her father and a grandmother before she really knew them. Then she lost her grandfather to cancer while she was still in elementary school. We had prayed so fervently for Grandpa to get well and to come to know Jesus. As he neared the end of his life in the hospital, I decided to be honest with Casey and tell her Grandpa only had a little while to live.

I expected our conversation to bring tears, but I was met with a stoic silence. I let her process the information for a while. Then with the bravery and innocence of a child, she spoke up, "Well, Mommy, we need to get to the hospital. I need to go see Grandpa and talk to him!"

So off we went. As we entered the hospital room, Grandpa put on a bright face and tried to act like everything was normal and okay, but Casey would have none of that.

After a hug and a kiss, Casey lit into him. "Grandpa, do you know Jesus as your Savior?"

"Well, yes, honey, I know Jesus," Grandpa replied.

"No, I don't mean do you know who he is. I mean do you believe he was God's son, and that he came to earth to die for us, and that he rose again to go back up to heaven so we can be saved and go to heaven to be with him? Do you believe he can save you so that you can go to heaven too? Because, Grandpa, I'm going to heaven, and I would really miss you if you weren't there."

Grandpa broke down crying and, through the tears, replied, "Well, Casey, I want to believe that. I want to go to heaven so that I can see you there. Can you tell me how I can do that?"

"Oh, Grandpa, it's easy…but it's not so easy too. You see, you need to ask him to come into your heart. He's just waiting for you to ask him. But the not-so-easy part is that when you ask him into your heart and he comes in, then you *want* to choose to obey him and try to do things right, and you're really sorry for when you do things wrong, and you ask him for forgiveness. And then he does forgive you. The really, really hard part is that sometimes you want to do wrong things, and you have to fight it! You can't just ask Jesus into your heart, but tell him that you'll obey him later. You have to want to start obeying him now because you love him."

Grandpa was sobbing at this point. He picked up her hand and asked, "How do I ask Jesus into my heart?"

Casey replied, "Oh, Grandpa, that's the real easy part. My Sunday school teacher says you just ask him, but let me tell you a secret, Grandpa. He's standing right outside your heart, and he's really the one who is asking you to let him come in. You just need to say yes! Just close your eyes, and I'll help you."

I stood there stunned with tears running down my face as Casey led Grandpa in prayer. He repeated each phrase after her. When she finished, she was completely dry-eyed and beaming as she said, "Grandpa, you should feel a real peace in your heart now, and that's Jesus! I'm so glad you told him you wanted him in your heart. I'm so glad I get to see you in heaven. So don't you worry now, Grandpa, Jesus is going to be with you, and I'll see you soon."

She kissed him goodbye with both Grandpa and me barely able to catch our breath in between sobs. She gave him one last beatific smile and left the room, waving. Grandpa died that night.

The tears came the next day. Casey laid her head in my lap and kept saying over and over how much she would miss Grandpa. I was asked to give the eulogy at the funeral home since Grandpa never went to church. I was shocked when over two hundred and fifty people crowded into the room for the service. I had decided if Casey could have the courage to talk about Jesus, then I could too. I told the crowd about Casey's visit and her conversation with Grandpa on her last visit with him. There was not a dry eye in the room, except Casey's.

*****

Middle school years brought its own set of problems with the onset of puberty. We experienced our second long separation when she trained for three weeks in Moscow with the Russian Olympians. The separation was excruciating for me, but Casey had a blast.

And there were a couple of her high school years when I wondered if an alien had come to visit. I remembered asking myself, "Where is my daughter and what have you done with her?"

Yet the journey was delightful. Even when life was complicated, it was pure joy each time I looked at my daughter. History was being made.

High school graduation came all too soon, and I paid her back for all the times she embarrassed me when she was a small child. She had a crush on one of the most popular boys in high school, Steve. She even went to prom that year with him. She had known him for years, and he went to our church. I was aware that Casey had never experienced her first kiss (unless you count the kiss at the airport when she was a twenty-month-old floozy). After the graduation ceremony and everyone was taking pictures and videos, I asked Steve to come over so that I could film him with Casey. He placed his arm around Casey and posed for the video. While I was filming, I spoke up, "Steve, Casey has never had her first kiss. Would you honor her with one tonight?"

Without hesitation, Steve laid a big one on her. Casey was so embarrassed that it took her over a week to forgive me. But it was worth it!

She was going off to college, and I would have to find my own life once again, as would she. And she did. She went far away to a university across the country on a gymnastics scholarship. She grew up and would now learn to make her own decisions and mistakes, but now, I wouldn't be there to walk with her. For the first few weeks, all I could do was cry. Both of us had many adjustments to make to become the healthy adults we needed to be.

*****

My daughter's childhood was rich in love, rich in experiences, and rich in time spent together with me. But my daughter's childhood was also a rich healing balm for me. I learned to trust. I learned to risk and to laugh at myself. I learned it was okay to fail sometimes. I learned I don't have to be the best at something to have someone love you. I learned that people you care about may hurt you, but that's okay...they are just people too. I learned to forgive...really forgive. I learned that laying my life down for another can bring the greatest joy and satisfaction. And I learned to love...to really love.

Loving people did not come naturally to me. I didn't feel I learned it as a child. Unconditional love was not something I had experienced much. I had built up so many walls to protect myself when I was younger; it was difficult to let people in. There was a hard shell around me that I covered with pride and anger. And learning to love was not to be an easy process for me. It was humbling.

My first real lesson in loving came after graduate school. I was in my first job, and my boss was a wonderful Christian man. It was the end of my first year of work, and I had to meet with him for the review process. Being the consummate overachiever, I was unsurprised at first when we sat down to review the four-page document. The first three pages were filled with "excellents" and "very goods." But then we got to the last page. It had to do with personality and ability to work well with others. It was a whole page of feedback from those with whom you worked, as well as your boss. "Hard to get along with, always angry, don't know whether to talk to her or not, can't tell which side of the bed she woke up on, does very good work, but is a loner. Does not know how to give credit to others."

I was mortified, and for the first time in many, many years, I broke down and cried in front of someone. I was so humiliated, but my boss had great compassion.

I will never forget his words to me. "Anne, I know you believe in Jesus. I know you go to church. You probably know Scripture. But let me ask you this. Have these phrases ever hit home to you? 'God is love. They will know you are mine by the love that you show them. If you love me, you will obey my commandments.' Anne, do you know how to love?"

"Obviously not," I responded tearfully.

He graciously replied, "Then let me have the honor of teaching you how to love others. You are a good worker, and you seem to have a good heart. Let me teach you what it means to have God's love for others in your heart. If you are willing to meet with me each weekday morning at seven o'clock, we will explore together what God's Word has to say about love."

I agreed to that offer, and it changed my life. For five months, I met with him, and I never looked back. I was twenty-four years old when I began, but new beginnings can be hard. That night after work, I went back to my apartment and fell on my knees. My heart was broken. I wasn't good at something, a *big* something—loving other people! I had no idea where to begin. I felt so broken. All I knew to do was cry out to God to help me. For two hours, I cried until I could barely breathe from my sinuses being so stuffed up, but I felt cleansed. I felt God's presence like never before. I knew this was a new adventure. And once again, I had to trust God…and eventually trust others.

During this time of growth, most of all, I came to understand how much God loves me. I became acutely aware that what I learned as a child was very true: God *is* love! He is all the attributes of love mentioned in 1 Corinthians 13. He is patient and kind, slow to anger, keeps no record of wrongs, does not delight in evil, but rejoices with the truth. He protects and never gives up hope on us. His love always perseveres. His love never fails! God choses to love me each and every day, regardless of how I respond to him. And the stunning realization hit me…I am called as his follower to love others just like that!

After three weeks of meeting with my boss, those words of Scripture were suddenly coming alive for me! They weren't just words; they were his words of love and encouragement to me personally. Each weekday, my boss prayed with me, he taught me, he listened, he cared, and God filled my heart with love. I knew I could love because he first loved me. And because love began to fill me, I became a new person. I became patient and kind and slow to anger. I had a newfound humility and no longer had a desire to keep a record of wrongs. I felt an intense desire to protect, to hope, and to persevere. Through finding love, I had gained everything! I learned that love, many times, is a decision. Often, it was a tough decision. It meant risking. It meant possibly being hurt. It meant opening up your heart. It meant forgiving. It was scary!

That fear was almost palpable when I made the decision to call my mother and tell her I loved her. Those were not words we said to each other. We had had a contentious relationship over the years, and we had trouble relating to each other. But I loved my mother, and I wanted to tell her, and I really desired to love and understand her even more, so I called. I generally called her once a week. The conversations were usually generic banter and didn't last long, but I had determined in advance how I was going to end the conversation.

As we closed out the call, I said, "Momma, I love you."

She must have been stunned. She had no reply but to say, "Okay, goodbye."

I was heartbroken. She didn't tell me she loved me back, and it would remain that way for a couple of months. Each time we ended our conversations, I told her that I loved her.

Finally, she responded. "I love you too." My heart soared! Our relationship only improved from that point forward.

*****

When I reminisced about my own childhood, I often felt sad that I grew up without a father. Perhaps Casey will feel that way too, but we both grew up with the greatest Father there could ever be. He is the only Father either of us has ever known, and he has never let us down—ever. He has always been there for both of us even if at times, it was difficult to see.

169

Life may have seemed simpler when I was growing up. It was certainly, for better or for worse, more black-and-white. There were long sunny days when I just went for bike rides all around town, played until dark, and came home safely at the end of the day. Other than feeling alone, the worst pain I felt was when my feet slipped off the bike pedals, and my groin hit the cross bar of the boy's bicycle I rode, or maybe Momma putting the switch to me when I frustrated her too much, or maybe it was when my brother would make me so angry, I put my fist through the wall. Ah, the joys of childhood!

The anger and frustration I felt as a child has long disappeared. The struggle of feeling inadequate and different has abated. Replacing it is a sense of peace and joy. As I grow older, I realize how much I need to say things that might not get said otherwise. Each day has become a gift. Each day brings less fear or awkwardness when telling those I truly care about that I love them.

When I was younger, my life seemed like it was on remote control. As I grew older, it became easy to feel like I was drifting away, wondering what my purpose was or if I was too old to pursue dreams any longer. It was easy to forget sometimes that I can still dream, no matter what the age, and that I can still achieve some of those dreams. In a way, getting older has been good. I no longer have the luxury of being scared to follow my dreams. I don't have the time to waste being scared. There is a freedom to just follow and do…even if I fail or feel insecure. It's now okay, and it's even fulfilling just to try.

It was also easy to get caught up in the drama of life when you are young. As I got older, I had less difficulty filtering out what was really important. I learned to better identify what I can and cannot have some measure of control over. I learned to let go of the things I could not control. And there was real freedom in giving up that control and trusting God. It made life a lot easier and a lot less stressful.

*****

We all have a suitcase full of sad memories as we grow older, missed opportunities, broken dreams, and regrets. We all are often so busy trying to be right, to be strong, to be successful, and to be happy that it becomes impossible to try and be satisfied with life. As we grow older, we all sometimes feel it can be tougher to be happy. We are *not* the same people we were. We are not as carefree. Time and people become more precious. Loss seems to hit us harder. Dreams become fewer. Doors close, and opportunities can fade away…if we let them.

I have always reminded myself that I grow old when I stop pursuing my dreams! Yes, I miss being young, being able to do most anything I want athletically, having all the boys smile at me, have people in the grocery store *not* call me "ma'am." I miss thinking that everything in the world is still a possibility, feeling physically invincible. Those days are gone. Now I find great pleasure in family and friends. I find great joy in knowing my brother thinks I'm fun to be with, or that my daughter thinks of me as a best friend and loves being with me. My heart bursts with gladness that my husband likes to spend time with me, or that my family *might* not think I'm so weird anymore. I find great comfort in discovering other people really don't care all that much about my perceived failure. That frees me to not regard myself as a loser.

I miss friends who have died but feel so very enriched to have known them for as many years as I did. I treasure the friends I have, new and old! I wish time had not gone by so quickly. But each day, I know there is more to do, more to experience, more to love, more to give, more to say.

Because I don't know how many days I have left, each day has become more important. People have become more precious. Time has become an enemy that I have to make friends with each day. I have stopped living life as if the purpose was merely to arrive safely in heaven. Each day is an adventure. Each day, I want to bring glory to God. Each day, I want to choose to love others, even if they are not particularly lovable at times. I want to learn better how to give of myself, expecting nothing in return. I want each day to be dangerous and exciting and radical. I want to try new things and stretch my wings. I want to fulfill his great commission to share his glory with the world, whoever my world might be.

Now, too, I want to try harder not to make mistakes. I have less time to mend those errors. Age has given me a new perspective. I can finally go out in public without feeling I have to be perfectly made up...because it's quite obvious people just don't care much what I look like! That's a bit freeing! Now I can listen more, laugh more, and even cry more. Age gives a certain leeway to do those types of things.

I spent so many years trying to hide from people, trying to build up walls to protect myself, trying to act like I didn't care. Now I like showing my insides, and I like seeing other people's insides. No one has to entertain me. I'm perfectly capable of entertaining myself. No one has to make me laugh. I do enough stupid things to keep myself in giggles. The best gifts have become relationships...with God and with people, especially family and friends. When we are together, no matter where we are, it feels like home. And home is now a very, very good feeling.

Epilogue

When I was thirty-one years old, I was challenged by my pastor to read the Bible all the way through as a book, start to finish. I must admit that I had never read it in completion, much less start to finish. I had mostly avoided the Old Testament other than the many children's stories that had been gleaned from it. When I started reading from Genesis, I couldn't figure out why Scripture kept admonishing the Israelites to remember. It seemed this was a theme running throughout Scripture, especially the Old Testament. There were feasts and holidays set aside to help the people remember. They were commanded to teach the stories of the Israelite people to their children, as well as teach them the commandments. In effect, history was very important to them. History brought meaning to who they presently were, to their purpose, to their lives, to their future, and to their culture. And when I think back on my history, it too brings new meaning, new purpose, and a reminder of all the ways God has taken care of me, provided for me, and loved me…even during those times when I had turned from him.

So many times in my life, I have felt like Humpty Dumpty: life came crashing down, and I felt I was broken into so many pieces that no one could put them back together again. Rubble seemed to lay all around me, but I learned there is nothing too difficult for my Lord. Each time, the Potter would take these pieces of clay and put them back together again in such a way that I never could have imagined. I have learned that being broken does not mean being continually sad. Nor does it mean I am not a complete person with value.

There have been many broken roads in my life, but thankfully, they have all led me back to God. I have chosen to submit to his desires and plans for my life. I now know there may be tears, there may be grief, there may be loneliness for a while, but joy does come in the morning! I believe God desires that we be willing to be broken, that we be willing to trust him with our future. Humility, broken-ness, surrender, discipline, and giving up control go against my very stubborn human nature, yet these characteristics seem to be exactly what God is trying to cultivate in me.

I know that God created me in his image, and I know that all he created is good. I know he doesn't make mistakes, and that I am cher-ished just the way I am. It is easier to remember all these things when life is seemingly going well. But when I find myself wandering in my own deserts, I find it harder. I doubt anyone looks forward to going through those times of brokenness. It takes courage to give up con-trol, to give up dreams, to give up plans you had for yourself or for your family. It takes courage to live on the edge, not knowing what will happen but knowing that he has it all under control. It takes complete surrender on my part! Psalm 51:16–17 clearly reminds me that God has a special closeness for those with a broken and contrite heart, "You do not delight in sacrifice, or I would bring it: you do not take pleasure in burnt offerings. The sacrifices of God are a broken spirit; a broken and contrite heart, O God, you will not despise."

One Sunday, I sat in church as the pastor talked about the "Father hole" in each of us. There is a hole in each of us that only God can fill, yet the concept of such a hole is even more poignant for some of us. I grew up having no idea what it was like to have a father. I thought everyone else's family was perfect, and mine seemed so extremely imperfect at the time. The school would host father/daughter dances, and I would never attend. The pain of those types of things haunted me for years.

God became my best friend. He has always been so very real to me. At times, I have felt as though I could feel his arms around me. As I grew in faith, I searched the Scriptures for verses about the fatherless. I clung to those verses, knowing that God's promises are true. Psalm 68:5 told me that God would be a father to the fatherless.

I believed that. Yet at times, there still seemed to be a gaping hole. I needed some skin, as Casey would say! I missed the laughter, the play, the hugs, the kisses, the love of an earthly father. Even so, God continued to nurture me, to protect me, to provide for me, and to grow me.

And I did grow up, got married, and had my own child. But my biggest fear seemed to be coming true...history seemed to be repeating itself. My daughter too grew up without an earthly father. I shared with her all the verses I clung to growing up. I told her that like me, she had the best Father in the whole world. But I determined in my heart that my daughter would grow up knowing without a shadow of a doubt that she is loved, that she is special, and that God has a very special plan for her life. And an unbreakable bond developed between us that has carried us though some very difficult times.

A couple of years ago, my daughter got married herself. The excitement of the engagement quickly gave way at times to the stress of the details. One evening, the stress came to a peak. This joyful time seemed to be wrought with strife. As I listened to her cry on the phone, I couldn't help but visualize our Father desperately wanting to hold her in his arms.

I stopped the conversation and asked her, "Are you letting your Father be a part of your wedding plans?"

She seemed perplexed at first by the question, then I elaborated.

"God has been the only Father you have known your whole life. He's been with you since you were in my womb. Don't you think he wants to be intimately involved in this very joyous time of your life that he has prepared for you? Are you lifting up every little detail to him? Or are you trying to make these decisions on your own? Are you allowing him the opportunity to help you with the stressors of trying to please everyone? Have you made a list that you and Jon pray about every single day until you feel you have an answer? As your mother, I wouldn't want to be left out of the planning. It would hurt me. Are you delighting your Father's heart by letting him guide you and be a part of this joyous event that he has placed in your life?"

Whether it be a wedding, a divorce, a lost job, a feeling of despair, or illness, God intimately wants to be a part of our lives.

He wants to take the broken pieces and make a mosaic that is beautiful…one that—if we are willing—can be used for his glory. Never forget that God makes beautiful things of us if we are humble, willing, and ready to give up control.

That, in effect, is the great mystery. To gain true freedom, I must be willing to lay it all down and give up control to God. After all, giving him me, all of me, is the only real gift I can give him. Everything else is already his. So I determined on that day when I was twenty-four years old that my gift of thanks to God would be me, all that I am, all I ever hope to be. It's not always pretty, nor is it new. In fact, it is broken and scarred. But I have learned when I give my all to him, he fulfills my dreams more than I could have ever imagined. I hope I have taught my daughter that lesson. It made me so very happy when she told me one of her favorite songs I had written was "I'll Give My Dreams to You."

I would sit on Grandma's knee and dream of all I'd
  like to be,
A movie star, maybe travelling far, Oh I could surely
  dream.
Now I'm grown, but still it seems life is odd with all
  it brings;
I don't know where I'm going, but I know You'll be
  there.
Dreaming of the future, running from the past,
Searching in the present to find a little truth;
Desperate to discover a peace that will last, I'll give
  my dreams to You.

Life has now come full circle…my baby is having a baby! Perhaps the greatest compliment that I have ever received was when my daughter said, "Mom, I hope I have a girl so that I can have a close and wonderful relationship, just like we did."

She will be thrilled with a boy or a girl. That's the way parenthood is. She will look at that newborn's face, and she will instantly fall in love. Before that child is aware of her, she will love that child, just as I loved her. Now a new era is born. The words of Psalm 139 are brought to life again.

> For you formed my inward parts; you knit-
> ted me together in my mother's womb. I praise
> you, for I am fearfully and wonderfully made.
> Your works are wonderful; I know that so very
> well. My frame was not hidden from you when I
> was being made in secret, when I was intricately
> woven in the depths of the earth. Your eyes saw
> my unformed body; and all the days ordained for
> me were written in your book before even one of
> them came to be.

Her child's history will most likely be quite different than mine. But my history is part of that child's history. In the long run, the importance of history would seem to be less about the big events that occur and more about remembering the Father who is always in control and able to make good come out of any event.

When it's all over and done with, we choose how we recall those events, for the good or for the bad. I choose to see them as an adventure, leading me to my true purpose. What man may have meant for bad, God has used for good. That is the ultimate love story! Before we are even aware of him, he is pursuing us with a crazy love. It is a love that is completely out of our control and beyond our imagination.

As Casey would say, "All we have to do is say yes!"

About the Author

Anne Hope is a former Christian singer/songwriter who grew up in a small town in North Carolina. She received her graduate and undergraduate degrees at Wake Forest University where she also played basketball. She has been a college professor, a division I college basketball coach and college administrator. She has been active in Christian ministry over the years, including initiating campus groups of Athletes in Action, writing courses, music ministry, missions, as well as teaching and speaking engagements. She was a sports newspaper columnist early in her career and has, over the course of time, remained an avid athlete. Anne now lives and works out of her home in Kansas City, Missouri. She can be reached at

<<Note to Layout: Add book website when finished>>

CPSIA information can be obtained
at www.ICGtesting.com
Printed in the USA
LVHW030658160321
681657LV00009B/148

9 781636 302065